Praise for The Verbal E

"This book provides a friendly voice that will assist parents, educators, and other professionals in utilizing these techniques with children with autism. It is a must-have for anyone who knows, lives with, or teaches a child with autism spectrum disorder."

— Kimberly Barnes, Ed.D., CCC-SLP/L, Speech and Language Pathologist

"I taught a class on verbal behavior once a year for 25 years. How I wish I could have had this book during that time. It would have made my instruction so much more effective."

—John O. Cooper, Ed.D., Professor Emeritus of Education, The Ohio State University, Co-Author of Applied Behavior Analysis

"With clear, concise explanations and examples, heartfelt stories and helpful resources listed throughout, Mary has provided the community with a nice description of teaching verbal behavior. Every parent of a newly diagnosed child should own a copy of this book."

— Holly Kibbe, MS, BCBA, Establishing Operations, Inc.

"A succinct, intelligible tour of an effective intervention for autistic children through both speech and non-verbal communication. VB is a refinement of B.F. Skinner's pioneering work on language and operates under the conviction that expressive language is behavioral, rather than purely cognitive. Barbera takes Skinner's arcane language and renders it not only clear but convincing."

— Book review by Kirkus Reports

"*The Verbal Behavior Approach* is a wonderful book! I typically get glazed over with the intensity of ABA/VB. This was an easy read that provided clear-cut, practical information that families and professionals can effectively use."

— Traci L. Plunkett, mother of a son with PDD-NOS

"Using a behavioral analysis of language as described by B.F. Skinner, this approach teaches language across functions, which Mary explains with easy-to-understand examples and language. Written from the perspective of both a parent and a professional this book will prove valuable to a variety of readers."

— Catherine B. Doran, MA, CCC/SLP, Speech and Language Pathologist

"I highly recommend Mary's book. It is excellent! Although it's very short and easy to read, it seems to cover everything! I'm recommending it to every parent and professional I come in contact with."

— *Sharon Zamrin, M.S.Ed., BCBA*

"*The Verbal Behavior Approach* serves as a practical and thorough guide on the principles of using the Verbal Behavior Approach for children with autism… The information that is provided in this text is comprehensive, concise and practical."

— *Book review in* International Journal of Behavioral and Consultation Therapy

"An amazing book that combines detailed instructions for parents on how to get started using ABA/VB with a little bit of emotional support to let them know that they are not alone."

— *Trish Cuce, mother of a daughter with autism, Founder of POAC of PA*

"*The Verbal Behavior Approach* provides useful information and resources for immediate application, accomplishing the book's main objective, providing for rapid implementation of an AVB program."

— *Book review in* The Behavior Analyst Today

"As a dedicated and caring parent, Mary has demonstrated her commitment to all children with autism by writing such a thoughtful and useful book."

— *Rick Kubina, Ph.D., BCBA-D, Associate Professor, The Pennsylvania State University*

"An easy to follow guide that works. *The Verbal Behavior Approach* is motivation driven, creating the desire to learn."

— *Kathleen Ricca, M.Ed., parent of a three-year-old boy with autism*

"…[*The Verbal Behavior Approach*] is an excellent source of information on Applied Behavior Analysis and on Verbal Behavior… There are countless helpful and well-grounded suggestions for parents who are interested in using this approach with their children."

— *Book review in* Journal of Early and Intensive Behavior Intervention *by Mary Jane Weiss, Ph.D., BCBA-D*

"This book accomplishes many things that few such works do – it pairs sound research with concrete examples, is accessible to the expert and novice alike, and touches the heart without sacrificing professionalism."

— *Anne A. Skleder, Ph.D. Provost, Cabrini College*

The Verbal Behavior Approach

How to Teach Children with Autism and Related Disorders

Mary Lynch Barbera

with
Tracy Rasmussen

Foreword by Mark L. Sundberg

Jessica Kingsley Publishers
London and Philadelphia

First published in 2007
by Jessica Kingsley Publishers
73 Collier Street
London N1 9BE, UK
and
400 Market Street, Suite 400
Philadelphia, PA 19106, USA

www.jkp.com

Disclaimer
The ideas, procedures and suggestions offered in this book are not intended to serve as professional advice
nor as a substitute for consultation with medical and behavioral professionals. Only a qualified professional
who knows and works with a child on an ongoing basis can adequately assess and supervise a child's
program to ensure
meaningful progress. Neither the authors nor the publisher shall be liable or responsible
for any loss or damage allegedly arising from the implementation of any suggestions
or procedures outlined in this book.

Library of Congress Cataloging in Publication Data
Barbera, Mary Lynch, 1965-
The verbal behavior approach : how to teach children with autism and related disorders / Mary Lynch
Barbera, with Tracy Rasmussen ; foreword by Mark L. Sundberg.
p. cm.
Includes bibliographical references and index.
ISBN-13: 978-1-84310-852-8 (alk. paper) 1. Autism in children. 2. Autistic children—Language. 3.
Developmentally disabled children—Language. 4. Verbal behavior. I. Rasmussen, Tracy, 1958- II. Title.
RJ506.A9B27 2007
618.92'85882—dc22
2007006818

British Library Cataloguing in Publication Data
A CIP catalogue record for this book is available from the British Library

ISBN 978 1 84310 852 8

Printed and Bound in the United States by Thomson-Shore, Inc.

MIX
Paper from
responsible sources
FSC® C013483

I dedicate this book to my sons, Lucas and Spencer.

To Lucas who has taught me how to love unconditionally, to hope but not to expect, and to appreciate the small steps along the way.

And, to Spencer, who is a wonderful brother to Lucas, and the most sensitive, caring, and funny eight-year-old in the world!

Acknowledgments

I first want to thank my husband, Charles, and my son, Spencer for their love and support as we continue to muddle through our journey with autism. Thanks for allowing me to follow my passion to help Lucas and so many other children with autism. And thanks for loving and caring for Lucas as much as I do.

I also want to thank Tracy Rasmussen for helping me write this book. I met Tracy five years ago when she came to our home as a journalist through our local paper to write a story about autism. It was Tracy who first suggested that I write a book and agreed to help me. Without her gentle guidance and excellent ability to take my ideas and help me write them clearly, this book would have never been written. So, thank you Tracy for your support and encouragement, and for helping me get this book published!

I would also like to acknowledge and thank the hundreds of professionals who have taught me everything I know about autism, Applied Behavior Analysis, and Verbal Behavior, especially those individuals who helped create and continue to support the Pennsylvania Verbal Behavior Project.

Special thanks to Jessica Kingsley Publishers and especially to Helen Ibbotson who agreed to publish this book and worked hard to get this information out quickly. I'd also like to thank Dr. Mark Sundberg, Dr. Vincent Carbone, Dr. Rick Kubina, Dr. James Coplan, Dr. Amiris Dipuglia, Marie Lynch, Kathy Henry, Teresa Kwitkowski, Jill Mahon, Wendy Yourkavitch, Carole DeInnocentiis, Lisa DiMona, and Holly Kibbe for reading drafts of this manuscript and giving me valuable feedback about ways to make it better.

And finally I'd like to acknowledge and thank my son, Lucas, for allowing me to use him to learn how best to teach him and others. You are an amazing, courageous, and beautiful child who has touched the lives of many people. In your ten short years so far, you have truly made a difference in the world. I love you from the bottom of my heart.

Contents

List of Tables

Foreword

Mary Barbera has written an exceptionally clear and practical book for parents and professionals who face the daily challenges of teaching language to children with autism or other developmental disabilities. Her book has a solid conceptual and empirical foundation that is based on the principles of learning and behavior initially identified by B.F. Skinner. These principles constitute the core of the well-known treatment strategies of Discrete Trial Training (DTT) and Applied Behavior Analysis (ABA) pioneered by Ivar Lovaas. Behavioral approaches have been so successful that in 1999 the Surgeon General of the United States concluded that ABA was the treatment of choice for children with autism (Rosenwasser and Axelrod 2001).

Skinner extensively studied the topic of language, and in 1957 published the book *Verbal Behavior*. He said many times that he believed this book would prove to be his most important work (e.g., Skinner 1978). In *Verbal Behavior*, Skinner provided a detailed behavioral analysis of what constitutes language. The book is important because language is the most significant aspect of human behavior. Language allows us to communicate with one another, express our feelings, let our needs be known, form meaningful relationships, respond to what others say, and better understand the world around us. Language also constitutes the basis of education, knowledge, intelligence, thinking, and social behavior. In short, language is the cornerstone of human behavior. It should come as no surprise, then, that if a child fails to acquire language in a typical manner, he or she will face serious developmental and social difficulties.

Language delays and disorders constitute the hallmark of autism. These delays and disorders then have a direct impact on a host of other important skills such as intellectual and social behaviors. Thus, the most important aspect of any intervention program for a child with autism is the early development of effective communication skills. However, for parents who have a newly diagnosed child, the large range of treatment options and professional opinions on language intervention are often overwhelming. Knowing what method or approach might work for an individual child is difficult for parents to determine, and valuable time is often wasted. Behavior Analysis in general, and Skinner's analysis of verbal behavior in particular, has diminished this problem by providing professionals and parents with a solid methodology for language assessment and intervention that has the backing of decades of empirical research. Mary represents a growing number of parents and professionals who have discovered the value and power of Behavior Analysis and Skinner's analysis of verbal behavior as a guide to the daily treatment of children with autism.

The basic components of the application of Skinner's analysis of verbal behavior or the "verbal behavior approach" were developed at Western Michigan University in the 1970s under the direction of Dr. Jack Michael. However, language is complex, and the early versions of the verbal behavior assessment and intervention programs were not designed for parents, but rather for professionals formally trained in Behavior Analysis. Over the past 25 years we have attempted to make the material more user friendly, but sometimes that is difficult for those of us who are deeply entrenched in the behavioral vernacular, and rely extensively on the conceptual tools of behavior analysis for analyzing and discussing complex human behavior.

While the basic principles and procedures described in Mary's book are not new, what she brings to the reader are clearer explanations, real-life examples, and a user-friendly guide through the complexities of this language intervention program for children with autism. While reading the book, parents and professionals will be able to immediately apply the approach with the confidence of the support from the well-established field of Behavior Analysis. Mary's unique perspective as a parent of a child with autism allows readers a first-hand view of the many obstacles faced by parents raising a child with autism, and working their way through the maze of "miracle cures" and intervention strategies. Mary is a registered nurse and her husband is an M.D. They initially learned about Behavior Analysis to help their son Lucas, but found it to be so valuable that Mary became dedicated to helping other families learn these methods. She became a Board Certified Behavior Analyst (BCBA), published empirical research on the verbal behavior approach, and now has written this book that clearly lays out the basics of the verbal behavior intervention program.

Mary's step-by-step descriptions of the teaching procedures and detailed examples will be a significant contribution to the existing material on Applied Behavior Analysis and the treatment of children with language delays and disorders. Her book is an easy read that presents a complicated set of material in a compelling fashion. Without question, this book will have a dramatic impact on a substantial number of children with autism.

Mark L. Sundberg, Ph.D., BCBA
Sundberg and Associates, Concord, CA

References

Rosenwasser, B. and Axelrod, S. (2001) "The Contributions of Applied Behavior Analysis to the Education of People with Autism." *Behavior Modification, 25,* 671–677.

Skinner, B.F. (1957) *Verbal Behavior.* New York: Appleton-Century-Crofts.

Skinner, B. F. (1978) *Reflections on Behaviorism and Society.* Englewood Cliffs, NJ: Prentice-Hall.

Introduction

I was a registered nurse with more than a decade of experience, but when my physician husband first mentioned the possibility that my then 21-month-old son Lucas might have autism, I was as bewildered and angry as any parent.

To be honest, I had very little experience with autism and it simply never crossed my mind that my first-born was anything less than perfect.

So what made my husband think that my son had autism?

He pointed out that Lucas wanted to watch television too much and didn't play with toys, and that, at times, Lucas simply appeared to be in his own world. At that time I wasn't willing to look at the possibility. I argued that Lucas had language, a good ten words, which wasn't that unusual for a child under two, and that he was a warm and cuddly baby.

He didn't look like he had autism, since he didn't fit the picture I had in my mind of what autism was supposed to look like. He wasn't banging his head. He wasn't rocking. He wasn't doing anything that I considered to be autistic.

I told my husband on that day that he was crazy for bringing up autism. I told him that Lucas didn't have it and that I never, *never* wanted to hear the word "autism" again.

Little did I know that a little over a year later autism and its various treatments would begin to take over my life.

Soon after my husband used the "A" word, I reluctantly had to admit to myself that I didn't really know what autism looked like in a baby. I had to tell myself that, as a physician, my husband might have a better ability than I to gauge Lucas's behaviors against other kids his age.

So my husband's comment did plant a seed as I began to carefully watch Lucas interact (or fail to interact) with the world around him. I thought about autism every time Lucas did something odd. If he took toys and methodically moved them from one basket to another I wondered, maybe…

If he played with a piece of string hanging from a chair for more than a few seconds I worried, maybe…

The word autism, autism, autism would spin around my brain only to be explained away by my desire to have a typical child, not a child with autism. But, Lucas did have autism. And the fact that I stuck my head in the sand and was in denial about it didn't help Lucas get better.

In fact, it made him worse.

Lucas got further and further behind his peers in language until it was undeniable that he wasn't keeping up. By the time he was two-and-a-half, the other children from his preschool were running out to their parents and asking if they could go over to a friend's house, speaking in full, animated sentences. Lucas's peers were speaking in sentences and developing relationships with other children, while my goal at the time was to teach Lucas to say the word, "ball." At that moment, I started to realize that I had no choice but to get out of denial and into the reality of my son's life.

From that point forward, I was in my son's corner as his coach and advocate, as well as his mother.

The Importance of Early Diagnosis and Treatment

Once I got out of denial in 1999 it took several months before a diagnosis was obtained and treatment could be started. In retrospect those were precious months of learning lost to the slow-moving protocol of the system of diagnosing autism. Today it is not unheard of for some children to receive the diagnosis of autism at 18 months or two years of age, but back in the mid to late 1990s, very few specialists were willing or able to diagnose a child under the age of three. All research completed in recent years supports a previous belief that children who receive an early diagnosis and early and intensive intervention have the best long-term outcomes.

Even today with research proving that early detection and intervention is key, the majority of children continue to receive the diagnosis much later than two, mostly because pediatricians and parents are still not aware of the early warning signs of autism (see www.firstsigns.org for typical milestones and red flags for autism). To confound the problem, the specialists who are qualified and comfortable in making the diagnosis of autism in a toddler often have year-long waiting lists.

Had Lucas been diagnosed and treated sooner, the strides that he has made over the past seven years would have been accelerated and I would have learned about the best treatments sooner, implementing them more quickly.

But much of the research and materials have come out only within the last few years and these include the important work of Dr. Catherine Lord and Dr. Rebecca Landa to discern the qualities for early detection. Nancy Wiseman's book *Could It Be Autism? A Parent's Guide to First Signs and Next Steps* was also published in 2006, getting important information into parents' hands.

So instead of being diagnosed and into therapy when he was 21 months of age, Lucas finally got his diagnosis and began treatment in 1999 when he was three years, three months old.

And that began my single-minded pursuit of the best possible therapy for my child and how I came to understand and eventually consult about the Verbal Behavior approach.

From Parent to Parent/Professional

I have since learned that there was some treatment information available in the late 1990s, but I didn't know where to begin. I became the "gung-ho" parent sitting in the front row of every conference I could fit into my schedule. I began to read every book that I could on the subject and depended on the knowledge of the parents who had gone before me to help my son.

I found that I was learning so much that I wanted to help others. I became the founding president of the Autism Society of Berks County in 2000; parents came to me for help and support continuously. I didn't want to leave even one parent in the dark about the facts or the different types of treatment. For me, the best way to help Lucas and others was to educate myself. In 2003, I became a Board Certified Behavior Analyst (BCBA) and began to work in the field of autism, specifically using a Verbal Behavior approach. As the lead behavior analyst for the Pennsylvania Verbal Behavior Project since 2003, I've trained hundreds of people and have had the privilege of working with many children on the autism spectrum as well as some students with Down Syndrome, and other developmental disorders.

Parents come up to me frequently and ask me one simple question: Where do we begin? They tell me that their child is falling further and further behind. He or she is throwing tantrums, has no language, is obsessive about different things. Like me seven years ago, they don't know where to begin.

So, I devised a simple way to get them started. This book offers a simplified version of some very complex treatments that I believe both parents and professionals need now. I will give you the information that I give to parents and professionals every day, the same information that I would give to my sister or best friend if they had a newly diagnosed child with autism or some other disorder involving a language impairment. I will walk you through the information you need and give you my perspective not only as a parent but as a professional.

This book will offer a simple explanation of how to use the principles of Applied Behavior Analysis and the Verbal Behavior approach to help children with a myriad of issues, including autism, Down Syndrome, developmental disorders, or even simple language delays. Drs Drash and Tudor have also recently completed some preliminary studies suggesting that the Verbal Behavior approach might even prevent autism in at-risk infants and toddlers (2006).

Using the Verbal Behavior approach has become my answer when parents ask me, "Where do we begin?"

This book will answer that question with simple, clear instructions for you, too.

Everything in this book is compiled from information I've learned along the way from internationally recognized professionals such as Dr. Jack Michael, Dr. Mark Sundberg, Dr. Vincent Carbone, Ms. Holly Kibbe, Dr. Brian Iwata, Dr. Glen Latham, Dr. Ivar Lovaas, Dr. Richard Foxx, Dr. Bridget Taylor, Mr. Michael Miklos and Dr. Rick Kubina among many others. I've learned much from colleagues and parents of other children on the spectrum too, as we muddled through cases and tried to find a way to help each individual student. I've probably learned the most, however, from my son with autism, who continues to teach me each and every day.

CHAPTER 1

Starting with ABA

Lucas's therapy was initially a type of Applied Behavior Analysis (ABA) based on the work of Dr. Ivar Lovaas. In 1999, most parents (including me) were so impressed with Catherine Maurice's two books, *Let Me Hear Your Voice* (Maurice 1993) and *Behavioral Intervention for Young Children with Autism* (Maurice, Green and Luce 1996), that almost everyone who was "doing ABA" was using a Lovaas approach.

In 1987, Dr. Lovaas studied a group of 59 children with autism, examining the best ways for them to learn. He discovered that the group of 19 children who received 40 hours a week of one-to-one ABA therapy had the best outcomes. Of that group, nearly half (47%) became indistinguishable from their typical peers by first grade. This study was the first of its kind to give parents of newly diagnosed children some hope and direction.

A follow-up study by Lovaas and two colleagues published in 1993 (McEachin, Smith and Lovaas 1993) indicated that those "best outcome" children in the original study maintained their abilities at age 13. These children continued to be indistinguishable in regular education classrooms without the need for an aide or other special education services. After reading about the Lovaas studies, I decided that ABA would give us the best shot at helping Lucas. It was important for me to find the best treatment for my child, just as I would have, had he had a physical disease such as leukemia. I knew that even if the chance of a cure was low, I'd still want the therapy that would give Lucas the best odds for a normal life.

The research on ABA goes much deeper than the Lovaas study though. With a generation of children growing up with ABA techniques in use, there have been hundreds of published studies that support it as a tool for teaching children with autism. In fact, in terms of research proven therapies, no other treatment even comes close to the success rates of ABA for children with autism. In 1998, Jacobson, Mulick and Green also published the results of a study, which showed that the Lovaas model of ABA was cost-effective in the long run, even though it is very expensive to implement short term. The studies showed that if the teaching techniques were used intensively during the formative years, fewer children required services after the first grade, through adulthood.

Unfortunately, the best treatment isn't always what children with autism receive. The medical profession may diagnose these children with a medical disorder, but the treatment for autism is usually provided by educational professionals who have their own ideas about what is cost-effective and appropriate—even if it's not shown to be the most successful. That's what happened to Lucas. In the United States, children with autism are entitled to a Free, Appropriate, Public Education, otherwise known as FAPE. Someone explained to me early on that Lucas was not entitled to "Cadillac" educational services but only to those comparable to a "Chevy."

Forty hours per week of one-to-one ABA therapy for a three-year-old is very expensive, and many educational institutions would prefer not to spend that money when other therapies (speech therapy, occupational therapy, eclectic special education preschool programs) are also considered "appropriate" by some.

My son's entire future was on the line and I was told to eliminate the word "best" from my vocabulary, at least in front of education professionals.

I did want to give Lucas the best chance at success by starting an ABA program for him, so we arranged for three therapists to work with Lucas as well as a consultant from a Lovaas replication site to come to our home once a month to train the therapists and me.

Because of that decision, Lucas made progress. I made progress, too, discovering that another form of ABA could offer even more benefit to my child. That's why this book is about that form: The Verbal Behavior approach.

The Verbal Behavior Approach

The Verbal Behavior (VB) approach builds on all of the ABA research but also enhances a child's ability to learn functional language.

VB adds an Applied Behavior Analytic approach to teach all skills including, most importantly, language skills, to children with autism and related disorders. Language is treated as a behavior that can be shaped and reinforced while careful attention is paid not only to *what* a child is saying but *why* he or she is using language.

The VB approach is a fairly new and popular approach that has actually emerged from the basic teachings of ABA, within the last 10–15 years. Although a relative newcomer to the field of ABA, VB is based on the teachings of ABA, but expands it to include B.F. Skinner's analysis of these concepts in his book *Verbal Behavior* (Skinner 1957).

Verbal Behavior is a very complicated book, which is probably in part why it was largely ignored for decades. It wasn't until Dr. Jack Michael and his Ph.D. student Mark Sundberg at Western Michigan University (WMU) began applying the concepts from *Verbal Behavior* to teach language to children with a variety of developmental disabilities, that anyone took notice of Verbal Behavior interventions.

The first few drafts of the VB assessments were created and tested during the late 1970s at WMU with much influence from Dr. Joe Spradlin from the University of Kansas as well. Mark Sundberg's doctoral dissertation, titled "Developing a Verbal Behavior Repertoire using Sign Language and Skinner's Analysis of Verbal Behavior," came out in 1980, nearly two decades before the Verbal Behavior approach became commonly used for children with autism.

It was not until 1998 with the publication of Drs Sundberg and Partington's three-book collection that parents of children with autism got interested in the VB approach. The main book was *Teaching Language to Children with Autism or Other Developmental Disabilities* (1998), but the most popular book in the trio was the *Assessment of Basic Language and Learning Skills*, most often called the ABLLS (pronounced "A-bulls").

The ABLLS can be used as a curriculum, an assessment, as well as a skills tracking form that consists of a series of boxes requiring completion by an adult who is very familiar with the child. The initial assessment using the ABLLS can take three to four hours to complete. Once you finish assessing where your child is with various skills, you then have to figure out what to do about it.

The ABLLS is a great tool for a consultant trained in the VB approach, but for a parent without any background in ABA, it can be very overwhelming. Although there was and still is a lot of parent interest in the ABLLS, the assessment forms can be somewhat daunting for most parents or professionals to complete. I've had several parents return the ABLLS to me without completing it stating that they just didn't understand how to use it.

By early 2000 enough people had caught on to this new approach, and its amazing results began circulating.

Parents of children with autism were traveling thousands of miles to hear Verbal Behavior lectures given by experts such as Drs Carbone, Sundberg, and Partington. After attending workshops and seeing videos of children making great gains with a VB approach, these parents were returning to their homes excited and empowered. They were purchasing the ABLLS and beginning the process of trying to learn how to teach their children. The popularity of the ABLLS and this new approach among parents led to a fairly significant shift for many programs away from a strict, discrete-trial teaching (DTT) or Lovaas approach towards VB. This, I believe, was due to the power of presenting this information and showing videos of children making progress directly to parents who were highly motivated to find out the best and quickest way to help their own children.

With DTT, the therapist presents a demand, gets a response and then gives a consequence. The instructor might say, "Touch nose", then, if the child touches his nose he'd be rewarded with a pretzel (or some other coveted item). VB works on the same principles of demands, responses and consequences, but the approach is different.

In writing their books, Partington and Sundberg's efforts to take the book *Verbal Behavior* and break it down into more common terminology with easier applications helped, but parents were still confused.

Two of the biggest misconceptions about the Verbal Behavior approach are that it is only useful for children who aren't talking, and conversely that it is only useful for children who can speak.

Neither is true.

Verbal Behavior includes all sorts of non-vocal forms of communication including pointing, signing, writing, or even gesturing. It even includes communication in the form of tantrums. The confusion comes from the fact that the Verbal Behavior approach is best used with children who are not yet *conversational*. This includes both vocal and non-vocal children. It's for this reason that the Verbal Behavior approach works for just about everyone with developmental delays. While most of the learners who use VB will be children, the techniques in this book also work for adults who are not conversational.

Improving Language and Reducing Problem Behavior

A Verbal Behavior approach almost always reduces tantrums and other problem behavior because it begins by assessing what your child likes and then uses those items and activities (called "reinforcers" because they reinforce desired behaviors) to motivate the child to do the work necessary so he begins to learn.

Once the reinforcers have been identified, the central theme for a VB approach is to teach your child how to make specific requests. B.F. Skinner called this a "mand" when he defined it in 1957 in his book *Verbal Behavior*. The mand is the centerpiece of VB programming.

With the reinforcers in place, the instructor can begin the process of teaching. Because the Verbal Behavior approach is very child-centered, it's important that the instructor be surrounded by all the child's reinforcers (the items that the child likes) and give the child "freebies" without requiring anything from the child. The child will learn to associate the adult as the giver of all good things instead of as a teacher who will make them do tasks they may not want to do. "Pairing" the table, instructors, work area, and materials with the child's reinforcers is the key in the beginning of a VB program. The goal is that the child will be running toward the instructor and work areas.

In the Verbal Behavior approach the child will immediately start receiving things and then soon will be asking for things (either verbally or using sign language). Eventually with systematic programming, the child will begin to ask for items that aren't on the table or anywhere in sight, either vocally, by using sign language, or less often with pictures. Once the child is responding to the reinforcers and asking for a several items or activities, the work is slipped in very, very gradually.

Incidentally, the Verbal Behavior approach requires relatively less documentation, making the instructor more available to be with the child, to engage the child, and to provide more learning opportunities.

Major Differences Between VB/ABA and Lovaas/ABA Programs

One of the biggest differences between the VB and the Lovaas approaches is that with the Verbal Behavior approach, expressive language is seen as a behavior that can be taught and each function of the word is taught explicitly. The various functions of the word "ball" for example would be taught by using verbalization or sign language. The child would be taught to ask for or mand for the ball when he wanted it. The child would also be taught to label a picture of a ball, to say "ball" when the adult said "ball," to touch the ball when directed to do so, and, finally, to answer questions about a ball.

In the Lovaas type of program, expressive language is viewed more cognitively and is not directly taught in the beginning with non-vocal children. Children who are not using speech when they start a Lovaas type program are usually not given another way to communicate initially. Lovaas consultants want to get the child to comply first with nonverbal requests such as imitation and matching programs. Children are rarely taught sign language within a Lovaas type of program although sometimes the Picture Exchange Communication System (PECS) is used if a child remains non-vocal after compliance is achieved. The different functions of a word are also ignored within traditional DTT, at least during the first few months of therapy.

Practitioners who don't use a Verbal Behavior approach tend to classify language as either receptive or expressive. You might receive a report that states that Johnny has a receptive age equivalent of a 2.1-year-old and an expressive age level of a 15-month-old. You might also be told that Johnny can say "ball," "cat," and "Mom," but these words are heard infrequently. This information, while providing some baseline information, is not very helpful in terms of identifying specific areas of this child's strengths or skills that would need to be taught.

In the VB approach, if a child is nonverbal, he is immediately taught an alternative communication system, usually sign language, to communicate his needs and wants, because, as noted previously, the ability to request (mand) should be at the forefront of his program.

If a child is not vocal, it is imperative that he or she be taught another way to mand so that the program can continue.

A Discrete Trial approach rewards children for complying and doing a lot of receptive language skills as well as imitation and working on matching skills, whereas with the Verbal Behavior approach a child spends more time working on expressive language skills such as requesting, labeling, filling in the blanks in songs, and generally learning to communicate better.

Both approaches work, but in my consulting practice I have found children and professionals more receptive to the Verbal Behavior approach. As with any type of program, there are great DTT or VB programs, consultants, and therapists, and then there are DTT or VB programs where critical errors are being made by well-meaning adults. The goal of this book is not to divide the autism or ABA community. It is my hope that this book will outline the VB approach so that parents and professionals have basic information about it and can begin to incorporate some of the information immediately.

I do believe that we owe a tremendous amount to Dr. Ivar Lovaas for his groundbreaking work using ABA with children with autism. Dr Lovaas gave us hope that children with autism could learn and developed the basic format for teaching them. Research in the past few decades in areas such as motivation, manding, verbal operants, errorless teaching, and reinforcement extend the work of Dr. Lovaas.

Some critics of the VB approach point out that since there are no controlled large group studies on this approach (similar to the Lovaas study published in 1987), we should continue to use a strict Lovaas approach for children with autism and professionals should persuade parents to stay away from VB. But this is counter-productive in helping children who can't wait 5, 10, or 20 years for large group comparison research studies to be completed. The VB approach is built on all the scientifically based research available and has dozens of individual and multiple subject studies supporting its use for children with autism. In my opinion, there is no reason to wait to use VB, since parents and professionals need to use the most up-to-date research available now to help our children.

Pitfalls When Not Using a VB Approach

When I initially consult in classrooms or in homes that are not using a Verbal Behavior approach, I see common errors. To be fair, these programs are most often not supervised by highly credentialed professionals; rather, by well-meaning people who are trying to do their best for these children, but are making critical mistakes. While the basis for DTT does include bringing a child to the table to do the work, some professionals or parents become frustrated with the crying or the tantrums and will reward a child for beginning a puzzle, while ignoring the child's whining. In this example the reward may actually be shaping up more negative whining behavior.

I've observed instances where the work is too hard or the tasks are too long and the reinforcement is too low. I've seen non-vocal children given receptive, matching and imitation skills but no expressive skill work, so they remain non-vocal.

On the other hand, I've also seen non-behaviorally based programs that are even more detrimental. The child may actually appear to be more content, but, without an understanding of how to get a child to communicate and what skills need targeting, the chances of developing a willing learner and documenting great improvements in language are bleak.

Children in these eclectic, non-behavioral programs are expected to learn with adults targeting complex skills such as prepositions, tenses, and perspective. For one completely non-vocal two-year-old, I observed programs that targeted skills such as pronouns (my turn versus your turn) and prepositions (put the bear "on" versus "in" the box). That same non-vocal child was given the direction, say "I want more blocks, please," when he couldn't say or sign anything. Clearly this child would fail in this atmosphere. Rarely are data kept in non-behavioral programs, and progress is usually slow and hard to measure.

Switching to a VB Approach

While I believe that the Lovaas type of ABA was very successful for Lucas, after six months of using this type of therapy day in and day out for 35 hours a week, a friend attended a conference where Dr. Vincent Carbone spoke about using a Verbal Behavior approach with children with autism. Using my friend's simple explanations, I began to move Lucas's program away from DTT to a Verbal Behavior approach.

I do know that having a Discrete Trial background was a huge advantage in moving towards a VB approach. Thanks to our Lovaas replication site consultant, Ms. Colleen Kline, I already understood the intricacies of prompting, fading, data collection, and reinforcement. In 2000, after hearing about VB, I changed agencies and began using home consultation services through Rutgers University's Autism Program in New Jersey, and at that point began to learn everything I could about the Verbal Behavior approach.

As noted, the VB approach falls under the ABA umbrella and is often easier for practitioners to implement than a standard DTT program. Many speech language pathologists (SLPs), who were trained using naturalistic techniques and often recommended that parents stay away from DTT, find the Verbal Behavior approach very easy to switch to or to incorporate. The terms might be new for SLPs, but VB therapy is usually much easier for them to begin to incorporate than the traditional type of DTT therapy.

That's not to say implementing a VB program is easy. In fact, the Verbal Behavior approach can be very complicated and it is often necessary to have a Board Certified Behavior Analyst (BCBA) or an Associate Behavior Analyst (BCaBA) with Verbal Behavior expertise to train your staff of therapists, to update the programming, and to revise it based on your child's progress.

The cost of these consultants can be prohibitive for families already stressed by the financial implications of autism, and while a BCBA with VB expertise might be necessary to provide ongoing training and to update programming in a state-of-the-art VB program, it is possible to put together a simpler program that will get you started and allow you to see the results of this approach. This more simplified plan will help you decide if the VB approach is right for your child, or give you time to begin a program if no BCBA or BCaBA is available.

VB information has been available, but it is somewhat complicated and difficult to understand. In fact, I found as I learned about this technique and, several years later, after I became a BCBA, that the VB approach could be broken down into simple steps that will give parents—and professionals—a clear understanding of how to implement a Verbal Behavior program to help a child with autism or with any developmental disorder or delay.

Although it may be a newer concept, VB is not a fad. It's based on scientific principles and agrees with all of B.F. Skinner's teachings on ABA, but actually enhances it by including his analysis of Verbal Behavior.

As a behavior analyst, I go into classrooms now and set up ABA/ Verbal Behavior programming for children as young as three years old in preschool. I've also been asked to privately evaluate babies as young as eight months old whose parents suspected autism, and I was able to offer them some suggestions for teaching a very young child using the Verbal Behavior approach. I recommended strategies to help engage the child and enrich his or her environment, and to find out what the child likes to reinforce the learning. So it's never too early to start with some of the techniques offered in this book.

I've also developed programming for children who are 10, 15, and 20 years old who have benefited from using this newer type of an ABA approach.

In my opinion as a BCBA and the mother of a ten-year-old son with autism, the Verbal Behavior approach is by far the best approach for non-conversational children with autism, Down Syndrome, or other developmental disorders. Although solidly a behavioral approach, it allows for the child to lead the way to his own learning by using things that he finds motivating. The child's communication abilities are clearly broken down into functional slices, making his language easy to assess and program for. Language and behavior are treated simultaneously as two sides of the same coin.

In addition to teaching the child to request (mand) and some other generalization skills in the natural environment, the child in a VB program also eventually spends a significant percentage of time at the table so the child gets the repetition needed to learn. The VB approach does use Discrete Trial Teaching, but ultimately combines everything that is great about that approach and makes it mobile. It allows you to work with your child at home, in restaurants, and in the grocery store. And it allows therapists and professionals to work with your child in the same way that you'll be working with your child.

Everyone who works with the child works from the same set of criteria, using the same motivators for the child and working on the same set of goals. Because of this, the child can and will make progress.

The Verbal Behavior approach also has a method for documenting and monitoring a child's progress so that you'll know when to switch targets and programs to keep your child moving forward. Overall, the documentation is not overly cumbersome, so you'll have plenty of time to engage the child.

The Verbal Behavior Approach is written to further break down the components of ABA and Verbal Behavior so that anyone can begin to incorporate Verbal Behavior strategies to increase the effectiveness of their programming.

This book was designed to help parents looking for a way to begin, or a new direction in which to move. It will offer a resource for caregivers of early learners and those with behavioral challenges. It's my hope that parents as well as professionals will increase their knowledge of ABA and the Verbal Behavior approach so that they can more effectively help their children.

So, let's begin.

CHAPTER 2

The ABCs of ABA

Johnny is three years old and difficult to handle. When you take him to public places he attempts to bite his siblings and throws himself to the ground every time he doesn't get his way. Johnny does have about five words, but he doesn't use them appropriately and instead repeats them over and over.

Johnny has been diagnosed with autism and you are frustrated.

The truth is, so is he.

Johnny may have a few words but he doesn't know how to use them, or any other means, to ask for what he wants, so he's miserable.

You have no idea how to get his problem behaviors under control, much less how to begin teaching him anything.

The average parent will attempt to discipline children using an arsenal of tools that includes time outs, counting to three, making threats, yelling, saying no, bribing the child into compliance (if you get into the car, I will give you a lollipop), or removing the child from the situation.

And so many parents are stunned when the behaviors (even the behaviors of typical children) continue or, in some cases, get worse.

The reason for this is that children use behavior as communication. Once you learn the language of their behavior, you'll be able to employ strategies to decrease the problem behaviors and increase good behaviors.

It's as easy as A B C. That is, the ABCs of Applied Behavior Analysis (ABA).

Before you begin any treatment plan you must be able to understand the function of your child's behavior. What is he trying to tell you? Once you are able to analyze the function of your child's behavior, you will then be able to treat it.

Take a good look at your child's behavior. Now, if I offered you $1000 to have a "good" day with your child, one where there was no problem behavior, what would you have to do to make that happen?

Chances are you'd have to let him do what he wants all day. You'll let him play on the computer or rewind his Barney tapes 100 times in a row. You'll let him eat all the junk food he can, and chase it with the beverage of his choice while spending time alone or only with the people he chooses.

And in addition to giving him everything he wants, you'll also make sure that he doesn't have to do anything he doesn't feel like doing. No putting on his own shoes, sitting at the dinner table, washing his hands. You know that if you spent the entire day giving your child exactly what he wanted, while simultaneously making no demands on him, you'd *earn* your $1000.

That tenet is the essence of ABA and the Verbal Behavior (VB) approach. You need to start working with your child in a place where all the needs are met and no demands are made. Don't worry though, you won't be there for too long. I've seen very well-meaning parents and professionals ignore that starting place, and the results are disastrous for both the child and the professionals.

Of course it's nearly impossible to have an entire day full of reinforcement with no demands, but, if nothing else, remember that if your child loves computers and hates math, you're going to get better behaviors more quickly from him if you start with using the computer. Once your child is enjoying his computer, you can then ease in the demands of math. Most behavior analysts want to know when the problem behavior is occurring. While this is important, I also always ask *where* and *at what times* the problem behavior *never* occurs so we know where to start.

The fact is that children with autism use behavior as a language and, until you understand theirs, they aren't going to use yours.

Let's use the example of biting.

If Johnny is biting, you will need to look at why he is biting. What is his payoff?

Sometimes Johnny may bite because he wants something he can't have and doesn't have the words to ask for it. But sometimes he bites because he wants to get out of doing a simple task, like hanging up his coat or taking off his shoes.

Johnny's biting, therefore, has two distinct functions. One is to get something he wants, and the other is to escape from something that he doesn't want.

Each of those instances of biting will need to be treated differently.

People often implement the same strategy for biting or screaming in general. Whenever Johnny bites he gets a two-minute time out.

However, if you look at why Johnny is biting, you'll see that placing him in a time out will sometimes get him exactly what he wants—to get away from something that he doesn't want to do.

Even if you eventually make Johnny complete the task demand, the biting was still reinforced because it caused a delay in the task. Johnny will most likely continue to use biting behavior to get out of or delay tasks because, quite simply, it worked.

If you have a child who is screaming or biting and has little to no language you want to get your child's behavior under control so that you can begin to teach him.

Don't worry if it seems overwhelming. This chapter is going to teach you how to keep track of what causes your child's behavior and how to implement scientifically proven techniques to reduce problem behavior.

As you go through this chapter, please remember one thing. The laws of behavior are almost as certain as the laws of gravity: If you reinforce a behavior, it will go up, and, if you punish or withhold reinforcement after a problem behavior occurs, it will go down.

If you are dealing with severe negative behaviors or with a child who could seriously hurt others or himself, I would advise you to consult with a Board Certified Behavior Analyst (BCBA) with autism experience to help you conduct a functional behavior assessment and to implement a behavior plan. When in doubt, seek professional help in addition to reading this book.

However, in most cases involving tantrums and more minor problem behavior such as hitting, pinching, kicking, and even biting (especially if the child is young and small enough for you to handle), you should be able to do an assessment yourself and develop a behavior plan or begin to use some behavior intervention strategies without the need to hire a professional at this point. This book will be your guide to learn what you need to at least get started with getting your child's behavior under control.

Learning the ABCs

To begin this process you need to know that every behavior contains three parts.

The first is the antecedent (A), which is what happens just prior to the behavior occurring.

Using Johnny as our example, the antecedent would be asking him to hang up his coat.

Behavior (B) is what happens after the antecedent has occurred. You ask Johnny to hang up his coat (A) and he throws himself to the floor and flails around (B).

The consequence (C) of Johnny's behavior is that you put him in a time out and hang up the coat yourself.

It's the C that will most likely determine how Johnny will respond to similar antecedents in the future, and in this simple example it's clear that Johnny was having a tantrum because he didn't want to hang up his coat, and your intervention had the desired effect because he didn't have to hang up his coat.

This vignette illustrates what is called a three-term contingency and all behavior can be broken down into an A, a B, and a C.

Behavior is not an art. It's a science called Applied Behavior Analysis, defined by Cooper, Heron and Heward (1987), as the science from which procedures derived from the principles of behavior are systematically applied to improve socially significant behavior.

But you don't need to know a lot about ABA to implement strategies to treat your child's negative behaviors and get him calm enough to begin meaningful learning.

In shorter form, ABA is the science of changing behavior.

Everyone uses the three-term contingency on a daily basis.

If I say, "Hello, what's your name?" and a boy answers, "My name is Matthew," and then I say, "Nice to meet you, Matthew," that's a three-term contingency.

My question was the antecedent, Matthew's answer was the behavior, and my praise that it was nice to meet him was the consequence.

The antecedent is always the thing that precipitates or comes immediately before the behavior. The behavior can either be positive or negative. The consequence can also be positive or negative.

A positive three-term contingency is asking a child to touch his nose (A), the child touches his nose (B), the child receives a piece of cookie (C).

A negative example would be, you say, "Do the puzzle" (A), the child falls to the floor and screams (B), and the parent withdraws the request and says, "Oh, I guess you're not in the mood to do the puzzle"(C).

The consequence is that the task is withdrawn.

In the first example we see that the child is likely to follow directions again because he or she enjoys the cookie. However, in the second example we see that the child probably learned that by throwing himself on the ground or screaming, the request was withdrawn. That's how negative behaviors increase.

Collecting Data

Before you do anything else, you need to collect some data on your child's behaviors.

First, select one or two behaviors that you find troublesome, such as screaming, biting, or kicking. You'll need to count how many times per hour or per day your child is displaying a particular behavior so you know where you are starting. In addition to getting a baseline rate over the course of a few days, you'll also need to try to determine the function or functions of the behavior.

To try to determine the function, get a sheet of loose-leaf paper and make six columns (see Table 2.1). All the way to the left in the first colum, you'll want to record the date and time of each problem behavior. This will help you keep track of how often the behavior is occurring and if a certain time of day seems to be problematic.

In the second column you want to write the setting or activity such as "speech therapy," "playground," or "watching TV." The next column is for the antecedent; the direction or activity that comes immediately before the behavior. The direction "hang up your coat" or simply "turning off the TV" could each be an antecedent.

The fourth column is for the behavior. You'll need this to be very specific in order to gauge progress. Don't write something general such as "temper tantrums," write that the child bit, or attempted to bite or threw herself down on the ground. It could be multiple behaviors of kicking and crying and screaming, but it's important that you are specific in this column.

For example, if your child kicks, you'll need to keep track of how many times he kicks and how you are going to define a kick. There are no

Table 2.1: ABC Sample

Date/Time	Setting/activity	Antecedent (A)	Behavior (B)	Consequence (C)	Function ?
9/14, 9:15 a.m.	Grocery store/checkout aisle	Saw candy and wanted it	Screamed/dropped to floor	Gave her candy	Attention/access to tangibles
9/15, 5:00 p.m.	Dinner time	Called to table to eat with family	Screamed "NO"	Let her eat in family room alone	Escape
9/15, 8:00 p.m.	Bath time	"Time for bath"	"NO" and dropped to floor	Picked her up and carried her to tub	Escape
9/15, 9:00 p.m.	Bed time	Left alone for ten minutes to fall asleep	Banging foot against wall	Ignored her and she fell asleep	Sensory stimulation

right or wrong answers, just how you choose to describe an event. If you define a kick as a forward thrust with his foot that makes contact with an object, then that is what you count.

Since you're being specific you'll also need to have a definition for the behaviors that you're counting.

With screaming you need to decide what duration and volume of the scream counts as a behavior you will document. You might decide to record all screams that last more than three seconds or you might decide to only record screams if they are paired with flopping to the ground. You know your child's behaviors and what you find most troublesome, so start with those.

And then for the fifth column write what you did or the consequence that immediately followed the problem behavior. Did you walk away? Put child in time out? Tell him "No crying?" Did you keep the demand on? Or did you move your child to physically have him pick up his coat? These are all examples of what might go in the C column. Write down what you actually did, even if you know it was the wrong intervention. This will help you come up with the function or functions of your child's behavior which can be listed in the last column.

Determining the Function(s) of the Behavior

It may seem daunting at first, but recording ABC data is the best way to figure out what triggers your child's behavior and how he or she is using behavior to get the outcome they desire.

This observation period should last two or three days, so that you will have gathered enough data to implement strategies for the behaviors.

When you begin to analyze the data, you may notice that no clear function appears since there doesn't seem to be a trigger for the problem behavior. You may have recorded that your child fell to the ground crying during his favorite video, when no one was putting demands on him. In those cases, it's a good idea to rule out a medical problem as causing the behavior. This is especially true if you are noticing severe behaviors that start suddenly. Some children with ear infections, tooth pain, or stomach problems can display problem behaviors that seem to come out of nowhere. It is always best to check with a physician to rule out if behaviors are related to a medical condition.

Once you have ruled out medical issues, you can begin to analyze the data to determine the function or functions of the behaviors, which you would list in the last column of the ABC chart (see Table 2.1). This might be the most difficult but it's also the most important step.

Children with autism and people in general have three main functions for their behavior: They want to get something, get out of something, or are simply looking for sensory input.

A behavior designed to attain something (a tangible item or your attention) would be screaming and hitting in the candy aisle of the grocery store. So if you look at your ABC data and it says, "He wanted the Barney video and I told him no," or, "He wanted the computer on and it shut off," or, "I was on the phone and she came up and started hitting me," those are all behaviors that are most likely used to get your attention and/or to gain access to something. The behavioral term for this function is "socially mediated positive reinforcement." The first part—socially mediated—means that a person or people are involved and the second part—positive reinforcement—means that the child wants something added (watching Barney, using the computer, or gaining your attention in the examples above) that serves as a reinforcer for the problem behavior.

Another function of behavior is to escape a task. If you analyze your ABC chart and you find a lot of problem behaviors after asking your child to hang up his coat or to do flashcards or to name items in a book, it's likely that your child is using the behavior to escape doing something.

You'll notice by looking at your chart that the behavior can be the same (biting) to get attention and to escape a task, so you'll need to come up with a different strategy for each of those behaviors. The proper behavioral term for this escape function is "socially mediated negative reinforcement." At least one person is involved with this function too, but the reinforcement the child is seeking is to have the adult remove something, like a task demand.

It's easy to remember the difference between socially mediated positive and negative reinforcement by noting that positive means to add something, like attention and tangible items, and negative means to take away task demands. Both functions involve other people (socially mediated) so we see these functions very frequently in schools, within therapy sessions, and in community settings. As we move forward in this book, I will use the terms "attention" (which includes access to things, too) instead of socially mediated positive reinforcement, and "escape" instead of socially mediated negative reinforcement.

The third function of problem behaviors is for sensory stimulation. Your child might bite himself because he wants input from his environment. Those types of behaviors are called "automatic reinforcement," and they occur when there is no one immediately around or when no one is engaging the child. These self-stimulatory behaviors often happen in all conditions, making it hard to determine their function. The child might rock or bang his head on the wall or make a humming sound. Sensory stimulation differs from other functions only because the behaviors happen when the child is alone or not actively participating in an activity or the behavior seems to occur at equal rates across all settings. The child could be sitting next to someone, but not be engaged by that person. All the child is doing is trying to get sensory input.

So now you should know what behaviors you want to work on, when and how often they occur, and what you've been doing to deal with them.

Don't be surprised if you see mixed functions for a behavior, as children will often use the same behavior to get a different response, but you should see a pattern. You may find that your child's behavior is 75 percent attention based and 25 percent escape based. Or you may find that 11:30 a.m. is a difficult time for your child.

You'll need to develop a strategy for each function of the behavior. Attention-seeking behaviors will be treated with one set of interventions while all behaviors which serve as an escape will be treated a different way. Finally, all sensory-seeking behaviors will be treated with a third set of interventions.

Developing a Behavior Plan Based on Function

Even if most of you reading this book are not behavior analysts and never will be, you can write a simple behavior plan yourself, based on function (an example of behavior strategies that can be incorporated into a plan is available in Table 2.2).

You already have the ABC written out and you have already determined that you have one, two or three functions for each of your child's problem behaviors.

It's best at this point to make a separate strategy for each *function* of the behaviors.

Table 2.2: Behavior Intervention Strategies Based on Function

	Attention/access to tangibles (socially mediated positive reinforcement)	Escape (socially mediated negative reinforcement)	Sensory stimulation (automatic reinforcement)
PRONG 1 Prevention strategies	• Pair environment/people with reinforcement • Eight positives for every negative • Set up routines and schedule reinforcing activities frequently throughout the day • Keep engaged with preferred activity when you are unavailable (set up video when you are on the phone) • Teach manding skills	• Reduce or eliminate activities or demands that trigger behavior • Give simple demands that you can prompt ("Wave hi" instead of "Say hi") • Set up routines so reinforcing activities follow harder activities (first bathroom then recess) • Pair work area with high reinforcement (TV, edibles) • Ease in work gradually	• Enrich the environment (music, color, toys, activity) • Engage child in preferred activities during day • Provide lots of sensory toys and activities (trampoline, swing, music, squishy balls) • Teach child how to mand for sensory activities
PRONG 2 What to do when the problem behavior occurs for this function	• Count and mand procedure • Ignore behavior/walk away • Short time out from reinforcement (with supervision) then redirect to a neutral activity	• Continue to repeat demand • Block access from reinforcement until child complies • Physically prompt, if needed and possible • Analyze after each episode to prevent future problem behavior	• Ignore mild behaviors that will not cause injury (rocking/moaning) • Block major behaviors • Wait five seconds until quiet/still then redirect to an activity and engage the child

You do not want to treat each behavior differently. You want to treat the functions of the behavior. So you'll need three different strategies: One set of strategies for attention-seeking/access to tangibles, one for escape behaviors, and one for sensory input behaviors. All behaviors that serve the same function will be treated the same. If Johnny screams, bites, kicks, and/or hits because he wants something he can't have, these behaviors will be treated identically. If Johnny screams, bites, kicks, and/or hits because he wants to get out of something, these behaviors will be treated identically. But each of those groups of behaviors will be treated differently from each other.

So basically you'll need only three strategies to improve behavior. One for all attention-seeking behaviors, one for escape behaviors, and one for sensory input behaviors.

You'll treat each function with a two-pronged approach. (See Table 2.2 for two-prong approach strategies for all three functions.)

First, you'll need to come up with a strategy for preventing and/or replacing the behavior.

Second, you'll have to write down what the adult should do when faced with the behavior based on its function.

The more time you spend preventing or replacing the behaviors, the easier it will be to get your child ready to learn. It's not unrealistic to hope to spend 95 percent of your time implementing strategies to prevent the behavior.

Whenever I see problem behaviors, I know that the demand is too high on the child, and/or the reinforcers are too low.

The child needs to be happy to work with the adult before any demands at all are put on him. And in the beginning, the demands need to be small—almost indefinable as a demand. Demands (that will be reinforced when completed) could be as simple as putting on shoes or getting in the car or saying a sentence. If you are seeing problem behaviors, step back and think about ways you can prevent these behaviors in the future. Simply put, to prevent the behaviors, you'll need to raise your reinforcement and/or lower your demands.

THE ABCS OF ABA   39

Treating Behaviors with a Function of Attention or Access to Tangibles

Preventing/Replacing Attention-Seeking Behaviors

Now that you are aware of your child's problem behaviors (because of your ABC list) you'll be able to begin by preventing the behaviors. For instance, if your child usually displays problem behavior because he wants something like candy when you go grocery shopping, you should try to prevent this problem behavior by making sure that the child gets lots of attention or, if he's allowed to have candy, you can buy him a lollipop on your way into the store and let him consume it while you shop. This way he'll already have his candy and will be happy. During the remainder of the shopping trip you'll be able to provide additional praise for good behavior.

Teaching a replacement behavior for the problem behavior with a function of attention or access to items is an important preventative step too.

The best strategy for this is to teach your child how to request things. Since requesting things is the centerpiece of the Verbal Behavior approach, it's discussed extensively in subsequent chapters of this book.

For now, you can help your child communicate and request things by pointing or using simple sign gestures. Make sure no one is giving your child things in response to crying or displaying other problem behaviors.

What to Do When the Problem Behavior Happens with Attention Function

For those occasions when you are not able to prevent the behavior and your child has a tantrum in the candy aisle, do not give the child the candy while she is tantrumming. She can have the candy, but not if she tantrums. You need to teach her this important concept.

Instead, stand your child up in front of you and say, "Susie, be quiet," and give your child the "shush" signal by putting your fingers to your lips. Then count from one to five (either out loud or silently). Then say, or sign, candy, and give it to your child. If your child is quiet for the five seconds then she may have the item, but if she is not quiet or starts up again while you are counting, you begin the count again, with the redirection to quiet and then the five-second count. This teaches the child that if she is having a tantrum she is not going to get what she wants, but if she can control herself and "ask" nicely, she may have the candy.

This is called "a count and mand procedure," coined by Dr. Vincent Carbone, and works very well for even typical kids to teach them how to ask for things that they are allowed to have. You probably want to teach this technique at home before trying it in public so if your child continues to scream, you'll be less likely to give in. Once you decide that your child will no longer hit the jackpot when she screams and begin to implement a count and mand procedure, you'll need to make sure everyone is consistent with this approach.

A count and mand procedure is actually a very short time out. Most parents and professionals who use time out often really don't understand that a time out means time out from reinforcement.

For children with autism and others with developmental disabilities, time out procedures often backfire. During the one-, five-, or ten-minute time outs, these children are not learning what they did wrong and what kind of behavior will get them reinforcement. I ask audiences to raise their hands if they think time out is a punisher and also to raise their hand if they think giving a sticker is reinforcement. Most in the audience think that time outs are punishers and stickers are reinforcers. This, however, is a trick question. We only know if something is a reinforcer or punisher if the future rate of the behavior being treated goes up (reinforcer) or goes down (punisher).

If you do use time out, make sure it is only used for the attention function of behavior because if it is used to treat escape-related behaviors, it will fail. Also, make sure time out is very brief (especially for children functioning in the developmental delayed category), and is truly working. Keep a record of how often you use time out so you can tell whether it is working. If the behavior you are targeting is not decreasing with the use of time out, this strategy is probably not the one to use. I usually recommend count and mand instead of time out for children with autism since you not only are teaching the child that problem behavior doesn't get them anything, you are also teaching them how to make an appropriate request.

I never use time out procedures for Lucas and have only used a true time out less than a handful of times for Spencer, my eight-year-old typically developing child.

If your child is asking for something that he cannot have, however, it gets a little more difficult. If Ted wants to go outside barefoot and it's zero degrees, you'll have to deny the request.

Here, the count and mand procedure won't work because you will not be able to provide the request at the end of the count.

Prevention in this case is most important. If your child wants chocolate, but is allergic to it, tell him that he can't have chocolate, but he may have an apple or cookie or something else he likes.

If that doesn't prevent the behavior and your child has a tantrum, the best strategy for this is to walk away and ignore the behavior. The child should also not receive the reinforcer that was offered before the problem behavior occurred.

If the child's behavior escalates, you should try to get him to sit quietly before offering another activity or item that he really enjoys. Again, though, don't offer the reinforcing activity until your child has been quiet for at least five seconds. If you start bribing your child with various reinforcers (items that he enjoys) during a tantrum, you will shape up that problem behavior. This is why it is important to separate the bad behavior (tantrumming) from the good behavior (asking nicely) by at least five seconds. If you are giving the child a tangible item or your attention (even negative attention such as scolding) while he is displaying problem behavior, you run a high risk of reinforcing and shaping up more problem behavior. If all of a sudden you see high rates of a new behavior, look for the person or people who are reinforcing it.

I see parents scolding their children often and know this negative attention is most likely serving as strong reinforcement. Think of the phone example: If the child is hitting you while you're on the phone because he wants your attention, then telling your friend to hold on while you reprimand your child is getting the child just what he wants—your attention. Next time, make sure he has something reinforcing to do while you're on the phone, if possible, and keep your phone calls short. If you must stay on the phone for long periods, pause when your child is being good and pat him on the back, give him a smile or a thumbs-up.

Treating Escape-Related Behaviors
Preventing and/or Replacing Behavior

If the child is having a lot of escape-motivated behaviors, think about ways you can increase the reinforcement of the table, people, building, and/or classroom. A portable DVD player, candy, and spin toys brought to the work area to entice the child to come may be a first step towards pairing the area with reinforcement. This reinforcement, however, needs to be at the table *before* the problem behavior starts. Stop calling the child to do work and simply play the DVD with their favorite movie at the work area. When they come to the table, let them watch the DVD and pair your voice by narrating the scene every now and then. Remember, you want to spend 95 percent of your time preventing the problem behavior.

If your child is using behavior to escape tasks or activities, it's important to lower all demands before problem behaviors occur, thereby preventing or reducing the behavior.

If you note that asking your child to do a puzzle causes a tantrum, next time try asking him to only put one piece into the puzzle. If he doesn't want to hang up his coat, the next time you come in you may ask him to take off his coat and hand it to you. Or you may decide that the goal for now is to have your child pull across a Velcro strap on his shoe, instead of making him put the whole shoe on.

Don't set the goal too high because it will likely trigger the behavior you are trying to avoid. And, as your child becomes more comfortable with what is expected of him, he will begin to do more.

The point is to slip in the demands so gradually that he won't know he is "working."

Replacement behaviors for this function include teaching a child to be able to ask for a break or help if the work is too hard, or signal they are all done instead of having a tantrum.

In the Verbal Behavior approach we don't use teaching breaks to a large extent because we want the child to want to be with us and want to be at the table or in the work area with us. If a child is large and/or the behaviors are very severe, however, teaching the child to say or sign "break" or "stop" might be the best option.

What to Do When the Behavior Occurs and the Function is Escape

It's been my experience that escape behaviors occur when the work is too hard or the reinforcement is too low. By working at the child's skill level you will be able to gauge what is too difficult for him, or if your reinforcers aren't strong enough.

However, if a tantrum follows the giving of a direction (such as "put a piece in the puzzle") you need to keep the demand on, and physically help your child do it, if you can. Whenever possible, give your child demands with which you can help him comply. Instead of asking your child to "Say hi," ask him to "Wave hi." That way, if he doesn't want to comply and starts to have a tantrum, you'll be able to help wave his hand, followed by reinforcement (of course waiting for at least five seconds of good behavior before reinforcing). Helping your child complete the demand is called "prompting." When you are beginning your program with your child it is imperative that you make demands that can be prompted, if your child fails to comply.

Generally, giving directions involving motor movements such as "do the puzzle," "clap your hands," "match apple" are easy to prompt. Telling a child to say something, especially if speaking is not a skill that comes easily, is almost always a losing battle since it is impossible to force anyone to say anything.

Once you have prompted the child, you need to think about why the problem behavior occurred. Be the "Monday Morning Quarterback" after every tantrum. In some cases, it is not possible or recommended to physically prompt children especially if it involves force of any kind. So, if Ted drops to the floor and he weighs 100 pounds, it is not recommended that you attempt to pick him up or move him to the table. If you or the child are in danger of getting hurt, it is not recommended that you physically prompt a child. Also, in some schools and placements, any pulling that involves more than equal and opposite pressure is considered a restraint. If you are in a situation that would require force to move or prompt a child, just keep the demand on, repeating the instruction over and over in a calm voice and blocking the child's access to reinforcement until the child complies.

Many children with autism will have both functions (problem behavior for access to tangibles and escaping a task) simultaneously. For example a child may have trouble transitioning from things he likes doing, to things he doesn't like doing; such as turning off *Barney* and going to the table to work. In essence the child throws himself to the ground because *Barney* was turned off on the television and he wants it back on (access to tangibles) and he doesn't want to do the work at the table (escape).

If your child shows problem behavior during transitions the best strategy is to prepare the child for the transitions. Don't signal that it's time for work and then turn off the television show (which could well be his favorite reinforcer).

Instead, you want to bring the reinforcer to the table or the work to the child so that you are able to slowly ease in small demands until you can turn off the television (or remove the toy, or stop the puzzle). This process will teach the child that he can give up the reinforcer, because it will be offered again in small amounts, incrementally throughout the work session.

Treating Sensory-Seeking Behaviors

Preventing or Replacing Sensory-Seeking Problem Behaviors

Sensory-seeking behaviors such as rocking, head-banging, thumb sucking, biting fingers, and moaning are common among children and adults with developmental disabilities.

Your child is most likely displaying these problem behaviors because he is not being as stimulated by people or their environment as much as he needs to be. Constant engagement of a child is exhausting and, in many cases, just not possible. Classroom staffing may not allow a one-to-one student-to-staff ratio and may focus too much on "independent work" to deal with less than ideal ratios. In home situations, it is also very difficult to keep a very needy child engaged at all times.

The two-prong approach to treat sensory input behaviors begins with a plan to prevent the behavior. This is accomplished by having a really enriched environment. You'll want an adult with the child as much as possible and engaged in something fun and reinforcing, so they won't need to look for sensory input. Have lots of sensory toys available such as a large exercise ball you can bounce the child on, a swing, trampoline, spin toys, and vibrator pens. Small sensory "squishy" balls are also reinforcing and provide lots of sensory input.

To replace these problem behaviors, watch for clues about what type of sensory input your child might need. If he seems to rock his body back and forth when he is unengaged, try a rocking chair since this is more socially acceptable and might provide great input. If the child is smearing saliva on table tops, try finger-painting or a Magna Doodle to replace the problem behavior with something more acceptable.

What to Do When the Sensory-Seeking Problem Behaviors Occur

If the behavior does happen, you may want to ignore it, especially if it is a mild behavior such as rocking or moaning. Another option is to wait until the child is still or quiet for a few seconds and then approach and redirect him to a reinforcing activity. For major behaviors such as head-banging, you will need to block the behavior either with your hands or with some physical device such as a helmet. As I've said earlier, if you are dealing with severe behaviors such as head-banging that could cause injury, I would strongly advise consulting with a BCBA who has VB expertise. This is an absolute must if you are considering using a helmet or other mechanical device to try to keep the child safe. When in doubt, seek help!

I hope that these behaviors will diminish as the child's environment is enriched. However, if that doesn't happen and the behaviors are severe and could cause injury, you'll need to consult with a behavior analyst who can help you to understand what is going on.

What You Should Start Right Now to Deal with Problem Behavior

You can begin collecting data on problem behaviors right now. Throughout this book, examples of problem behavior include tantrum behavior such as crying, kicking, biting, and hitting. You should always start by tackling problem behaviors that could cause injury to the child or others. But, even if a child's behavior is not aggressive or self-injurious behavior, if it is of concern then any behavior can be a problem behavior. I have tracked behaviors such as the number of times a child says "no" or "this is dumb" or "I can't do it." I have also worked on problem behaviors of children reciting scripts from movies, drawing on tables with markers, and sticking their hands down their pants. Obviously these behaviors are not going to cause injury but they still can be extremely disruptive and interfere with learning.

Get your paper out and start recording the number of times your child engages in one or two of his most severe behaviors by making tally marks on a piece of paper or, if the behavior of concern happens frequently, you should invest in a clicker counter to tally behaviors. These clicker counters are available at most office supply stores or at www.difflearn.com.

Next start jotting down the A, the B, and the C of your child's behavior (see Table 2.1, p. 34 for a sample ABC form). Analyze the data and, using the behavior strategies listed in Table 2.2, come up with a simple behavior plan to treat the behavior. Then distribute your plan to every person who is working with or spending time with the child so that everyone handles the function of the behaviors in the same way.

Although putting the plan in writing is good, you'll also need to show other caregivers how to recognize and react to different behaviors. Adults can role play with each other (one of the adults plays the role of the child) and make sure you watch others deal with your child's problem behavior while it is happening. Consistency is the key!

This means that everyone from the babysitter to your mother-in-law knows how to prevent and handle problem behaviors.

One caution: Once you start implementing a behavior plan, especially if the child has been receiving reinforcement for problem behaviors for months or years, you may see an initial increase in problem behaviors before the behavior gets better.

The behaviors might also begin to look different since, in the past, you may have ignored crying but may have responded immediately to the child being aggressive toward their sibling. While implementing a new behavior plan, don't leave a child unattended while they are displaying problem behaviors. Stay with the child to keep him and others safe since his problem behavior could escalate.

In time—a short time—you should see your child's behavior improve. If it doesn't you'll need to re-examine your plan, make some changes, and consider seeking professional assistance from a BCBA. This method is ultimately very easy to track if you took baseline data. If the behaviors go down or are eliminated shortly after you implemented a behavior plan, you've gotten to the heart of your child's issues. If the behaviors stay the same or increase, you'll need to revisit how you're handling things.

Continuing to track the rate of behaviors as well as taking some ABC data will allow you to see if the behaviors are increasing or decreasing. This data will also help you keep an eye on the function of the behavior as well as indicate to you if everyone is treating the behavior according to the plan.

Once you've got the behavior somewhat under control, you can begin to get the child engaged in learning. That will decrease problem behaviors even more because he'll finally be learning one of the most important lessons in life: How to communicate with language, not with problem behavior.

CHAPTER 3

Assessing Your Child

English teachers would have you believe that language consists of verbs and nouns and pronouns, while most speech pathologists look at language as either "expressive" (the ability to speak) or "receptive" (the ability to understand). While neither the English teacher nor the speech pathologist is wrong, as a Verbal Behavior (VB) practitioner I break language down even more, allowing me to fully understand a child's skills and to work on each area of communication separately.

To see how far you've come, you'll need to know where you started. I do that by assessing a child's ability before designing the program. If you build a pyramid on a base that is not solid, it will crumble. For this reason, it is important to start building basic skills before more complex skills can be taught.

B.F. Skinner suggested that talking is a learned behavior controlled by environmental variables such as motivation, reinforcement, and antecedent stimuli. If you talk, you will receive some sort of acknowledgement for your speech. If you think of a baby just beginning to babble, he or she will use lots of easy sounds such as "ma" or "ba" or "da," as well as open vowel sounds such as "aaaa" or "oooo." Since most parents wait to hear "mama" or "dada" as the first words, those babbling noises are reinforced. The open vowel sounds don't get quite the attention that a potential "mama" does, so they aren't as reinforced. When a baby makes a "ma" or a "da" sound, parents will be thrilled and shower the baby with lots of attention, including tickles and hugs and milk (which is a preferred edible for most babies).

This is how language begins to take shape in typically developing babies.

It is, essentially, how children with developmental delays also learn language, but with more obvious reinforcement since their language development is much slower.

Still, we are all focused on words. "Does your child talk?" is a common question asked of the parents of children with potential delays. The responses can vary from "not at all," to "it's inconsistent but some words are used," to "regularly using about ten words," to "talking all the time."

But having words is different than being able to use words effectively. A four-year-old child can be described as having an expressive age equivalent to a 2.2-year-old, and receptive language skills of a 3.4-year-old. It's just not enough information to accurately assess a child's skill level.

As a behavior analyst I need a lot more information about the function of a child's language. How does he use these words? When does he use these words? How often does he use these words? Instead of looking at expressive language as a whole, VB practitioners break it down into smaller units, including manding, tacting, echoic, intraverbal, and spontaneous language. You'll need to assess each of these skills to plan your VB program.

I've included an assessment form in the back of this book (see Appendix 2) that should be helpful in documenting your child's baseline skills across both verbal and nonverbal operants.

Assessing Manding Skills

My first question to parents is, "How does your child let you know when he wants or needs something?" What I'm asking, essentially, is, "How does your child *mand*?" Manding is the most important operant since it is always preceded by motivation and ends with the child receiving what he requested.

Scientifically speaking, a word is not a mand if there is no motivation preceding it. A child wants a cookie, so he mands (asks) for it. Skinner said that the motivation is often precipitated by satiation and deprivation. If a child loves potato chips and mands for them and receives them, there will eventually come a point where the child has eaten his fill of potato chips and will then mand for water or juice. He has satiated his desire for potato chips, but then desires water or juice. That exemplifies the motivation behind the mand: The desire must come prior to the mand.

Using the ABC example in behavior therapy, motivation is the A (antecedent), while the behavior is asking for the cookie (B), and the consequence (C) is a direct reinforcement (the child gets the cookie). As discussed in Chapter 2, any behavior that is reinforced will be maintained or increased. So if the child is reinforced directly after the mand, you can expect that the use of the mand will continue or increase. Your child will understand that when he says "cookie," he will receive a cookie. So when he's hungry he will likely mand instead of tantrum because that will be the quickest way to satisfy his desire.

When assessing manding skills, it is best to think about anything which is out of sight that your child currently requests without a prompt. For many early learners, the ability to mand for items is very weak, especially for things that are out of sight, so writing down the number of out-of-sight mands shouldn't take long. Once you have recorded all out-of-sight mands, next gather several of your child's preferred edibles, drinks, and toys. Present a small piece of cookie (or other preferred edible) for free and see if the child takes it and eats it. If he does, you know the motivation is strong so hold up another piece of a cookie and wait five seconds to see if your child says or signs the word. This will be recorded as a "mand in sight" if he vocally says "cookie" or uses sign language. If the child does not say or sign "cookie," present the verbal or sign model three times with about one second in between each model, like this: "Cookie"—one-second time delay; "cookie"—one-second time delay; "cookie." As you are giving the three models, bring the cookie slightly closer to the child as you say "cookie" for the second and third time. If the child tries to say cookie with a model, note this in the third column that you will entitle: "Mand in sight with vocal model." Continue this procedure to test the full range of your child's manding ability.

A typical child mands hundreds of times per day for many different reinforcers and then moves on to manding for attention such as "Hey look at me" and manding for information such as "Where is Daddy?" usually by the time they reach their third birthday. So, unless your child is a "mand monster," keep assessing until you have an exhaustive list of mands.

Assessing Tacting Skills

A "tact" is the next verbal operant. It may help you to associate the meaning of the word, if you remember conTact. When you see, smell, taste, hear, or feel something, you communicate by labeling—tacting—the item or describing it. Once a child can mand for several items, you can begin to teach him tacting. One of the best ways to introduce your child to tacting is to take photos of his favorite reinforcers and then ask him to tact the items. You could use the actual items, but I don't recommend it, as there will be confusion between manding for the item and tacting. Using pictures also helps the child cross operants more easily. The procedure for teaching tacts and transferring skills across operants will be fully explained later in this book, but for the purposes of understanding the different operants, just remember that a tact is labeling something that you see, hear, smell, taste, or touch.

To assess tacts, it is best to gather objects of common things and put them in a clear bin marked "tacts." You'll also need to buy some flash-cards, print out clip art, or cut out pictures from magazines to assess the child's ability to tact pictures. Assess tacting of objects and pictures by asking the child, "What is this?" and recording the child's response. If the child's tacting repertoire is strong, you can use first 100- or 1000-word books and point from picture to picture to assess this skill. If the tacting skills are weak, however, or if the child is distracted by several items on a page, you'll need to use flashcards.

Young, typical children build their vocabularies to thousands of tacts before reaching school age. Keep assessing tacts even if this is a strength, and keep going until you build a list well over a hundred. If the child has limited or no tacting ability you can stop after assessing ten items and pictures.

Assessing Echoic Skills

The echoic operant is fairly self-explanatory. It involves repeating what someone else says, similar to an echo. With typically developing children, the ability to echo is crucial to their learning. A typical child will see a bulldozer working on a job site and ask a parent, "What's that?" The parent responds, "That's a bulldozer." And the child echoes "bulldozer." Most typical children get the new word in one or two tries and then it won't have to be repeated.

A child with autism may have some language, but an inability to echo what another person says can stall that development. In some cases, a child with autism may not be able to repeat immediately, but will have a delayed echolalia, which also gets in the way of learning. Lucas had that, to a small degree. We took him to a museum right about the time of his second birthday (before his diagnosis) and were looking at the ducks. Instead of being fascinated by the ducks, he was fascinated by the signs prohibiting the feeding of the ducks. My husband and I took him from sign to sign, reading, "Please do not feed the ducks," and then adding "quack, quack." He would not repeat the phrase at the museum, but in the middle of the night he'd awaken and say, "Please do not feed the ducks quack quack." At that time I hadn't heard of delayed echolalia, and counted this as a bona fide phrase, taking it as a good sign that Lucas was able to put words together into a sentence.

To assess the child's echoic skills, make sure no materials or items are present and have the child sitting near you, preferably facing you. Pick simple sounds first to assess such as "Say ma" and "Say ba." If the child echoes simple sounds, move on to one-syllable words such as "Say cup" and "Say ball." Move forward to assess multi-syllable words and then phrases from there.

Echoics will be covered in Chapter 9. For now, just remember that the echoic operant is similar to an echo. The antecedent for an echoic is someone else's Verbal Behavior (saying a word or a phrase) and the behavior is when the child repeats the phrase, either exactly or approximately. It can be immediate, or delayed. Getting echoic control is another important step and can actually open the floodgates of language, since the ability to echo increases the ability to learn.

Children with autism often have no echoic ability, or sometimes they are able to echo almost anything so there is no need to assess hundreds of words. Instead simply assess the child's ability to echo simple sounds (ma, da, do), then one-syllable words (cat, bed), then multiple-syllable words, and finally sentences.

Assessing Intraverbal Skills

The intraverbal operant involves the ability to answer questions and is important in a child's development of conversation skills. Lucas did have some intraverbal skills prior to his diagnosis of autism. My husband discovered this ability, but neither of us was aware that being able to fill in the blanks to songs and nursery rhymes was an intraverbal skill. I remember one day when my husband told me to watch what happened when he began singing the theme song to the PBS series, *Arthur.* My husband sang, "And I say…" and Lucas would fill in, "Hey!" Then my husband sang the next line, "What a wonderful kind of…" and Lucas would say "Day!" They sang the whole song this way, with Lucas filling in the blanks. What was so confusing to me at that time was that Lucas could not say these words in any other context. If I said, "Say day," he couldn't do it. Neither could he ask my husband to sing the song, nor label or tact anything. He was just saying words that turned out to be intraverbals.

So, when I evaluate children who have minimal language I can often-times get them to fill in the blanks to familiar songs. The key to assessing this skill, though, is to sing a song that the child has heard many times over. Leave out the last word of each line. For example, when singing the theme song to *Barney*, you'd start off by singing loudly and slowly, "I love…" and leave the final word off. If your child doesn't fill in the word "You," then you say it, and go on to the next line, "You love…" waiting a few seconds for the child to fill in the word "Me." If he doesn't, then you provide it for him.

If your child is able to fill in one-word blanks in songs, the next step in assessing this skill is to see if he can fill in more functional phrases about daily life. In this case you'd say things like, "You sleep in a…" or, "You drink from a…" and see if the child can fill in "bed" and "cup." A child usually needs to master these types of simple fill-in intraverbal skills prior to being able to answer more complex intraverbals such as, "What flies in the sky?" "Name three colors," or "What fruit is yellow?" Intraverbals will be more thoroughly explained in Chapter 9, but at this point, remember that an intraverbal is an answer to a question that is pre-cipitated by another person.

Assessing Expressive Strengths as Well as Weaknesses

The four primary verbal operants are the mand, tact, echoic, and intraverbal. Together, they make up what speech pathologists call "expressive language."

I want to let you know now, that many children with autism or other developmental delays actually have scattered skills. When we started our first Lovaas Applied Behavior Analysis (ABA) program, Lucas already could mand for several items and, as illustrated above, had some intraverbal skills as well, but he couldn't tact or verbally imitate (echo) anything on command. Since I was not aware of the Verbal Behavior approach at that time, I was not using his expressive strengths as I do now with other children. Don't forget to assess a child's strengths as well as his weaknesses. Begin by documenting where your child is succeeding and don't worry so much about accuracy as intent. If you hold up a piece of a cookie, and your child says, "too key" or "ca cee" he is still manding for the cookie. Reinforce that behavior by giving him the cookie, but make sure to model the proper way to say it and write down the child's pronunciation of the word "cookie."

Also keep track of words that your child echoes. If you hold up a piece of cookie and your child says nothing, you say "cookie." Repeat it again, and see if the child repeats it back. Record this incident as a prompted mand since you provided the item and the vocal model.

And, keep track of the words your child will tact (label) when he sees either the real item or a picture. Finally, keep track of the words that your child is using to fill in the blanks to a song. These data will help you design a program for your child that specifically targets his weaknesses by playing on his strengths.

In assessing current skills, you'll also want to have an idea of how much your child is talking, even if it's just babbling. Set a kitchen timer for 30 minutes or an hour and simply count how many sounds or words your child says in his natural environment. This will also serve as your baseline prior to beginning your program.

Assessing Nonverbal Operants

Skinner does address the role of the listener in Chapter 7 of his book *Verbal Behavior* (1957), but does not address nonverbal operants such as receptive language. However, improving a child's receptive language is integral to any ABA program, including those programs using a VB approach. Most of the credit for defining and developing nonverbal programs goes to Dr. Ivar Lovaas and many other ABA practitioners and researchers that followed and replicated his important work. These operants—receptive, imitation, and visual performance—are included on the Assessment of Basic Language and Learning Skills (ABLLS), making these important components of VB.

Working with these operants will be discussed in detail later in this book, but you'll need to know a little about them to accurately assess where your child is strong and where work is needed.

Assessing Receptive Language Skills

Receptive language does not require speaking and is basically your child's ability to understand what is being said, so he can follow directions or comply with a request. Typical children who are simply speech delayed as well as some children with developmental delays actually have quite good receptive language skills. Many parents will comment about how their child understands everything said to them, and are compliant with requests. A child who doesn't speak may well be able to respond appropriately to the request, "Bring me the ball," or, "Go get a diaper."

However, children with autism sometimes appear deaf, because they don't react to requests at all. Some parents visit an audiologist before seeing any other type of practitioner. We took Lucas to an audiologist when he was two because he wasn't responding to his name. I remember thinking at the time that it would be horrible if Lucas had to wear hearing aids. If only his problem had been that simple. But even I noticed at the time that while Lucas didn't respond to his name, he did seem to have good hearing in other situations. He always heard the *Barney* theme playing in the next room. So, of course, Lucas's hearing checked out just fine. Now that I know more about autism, I can see that motivation to respond to his name was the culprit, not poor hearing.

One of the first directives given to us by our first consultant, Colleen Kline, on her first day of consultation at our home, was to stop using Lucas's name so much. In our effort to get him to understand and comply with tasks, we had paired his name with all our demands. So what he heard all day was, "Lucas get your shoes," or, "Lucas touch your nose," or, "Lucas come here." Since he rarely responded and we didn't know how to prompt him to comply, we would just get louder and repeat his name coupled with our demands over and over throughout the day. Colleen explained to us that Lucas needed simple language without the addition of his name: Come here, get shoes, touch nose. She also told us that we needed to pair his name with positive reinforcement instead of pairing his name with demands. For instance, we would use his name only when we were delivering food, drink, or fun activities. "Lucas, here is a chip, chip, chip," "Lucas wants a push, push, push," "Hip, hip hooray for Lucas."

The most difficult part of assessing your child's receptive language abilities is to continually make sure you are not prompting your child with the answer in any way, or giving him a visual cue. When assessing receptive skills you must keep your hands still by your sides, your voice neutral, and watch your eye gaze too, which could serve as a prompt. Give a clear direction: "Touch nose." If the child touches his nose, he has understood the request. However, if he touches his head first and then his nose, it is considered an error.

Typically developing children usually have intact receptive language abilities. Some children with autism such as Lucas have no receptive language skills when you initially assess them while others are almost age-appropriate in this domain.

Assessing Imitation Skills

Imitation skills should be assessed next. You'll need two identical objects of each: Cars, pencils, and cups. Put just identical cars on the table or the floor and tell the child to "do this" as you move your car up and back several times. See if the child does the same with his car. Next move on to the pencils by putting two pencils on the table and removing the cars. Take your pencil and tap it on the table, saying "Do this."

After you have assessed the toy/object imitation, you move on to assessing gross motor imitation skills. These are big movements using the arms and legs, such as jumping or clapping hands. A child should be able to copy your movements without your prompting (except to say "Do this"). Do not use phrases such as "Clap hands" or "Jump up" during this assessment. Only use the command, "Do this," to see if your child can imitate you. If you clap your hands and say "Clap hands," you will be assessing two different operants—receptive and motor imitation. During assessment, it is important to try to keep the assessments of these operants separate. Eventually your child should be able to imitate you with no prompting at all, but early on, children will need the direction "Do this." Like the echoic skills, I find most children with developmental disorders either have no ability to imitate or they can imitate almost any movement. Careful assessment is key.

Assessing Visual Performance Skills

The final nonverbal operant that you'll be assessing is your child's ability to match to sample or complete other visual performance skills. Many children with autism are visual learners, so it does make sense that matching should be a skill at which they excel and enjoy. In a VB approach, matching is usually introduced right after the child learns to mand for a few items but can be started even earlier during the pairing process if the child likes matching and puzzle activities. "Puzzle" is often one of the first mands taught to students who are strong visual learners.

Matching skills require some supplies. You'll need to gather identical objects from around your home. These could include identical plastic forks, baby shoes, number 2 pencils, plastic plates, kiddie meal toys (it's easy enough to get duplicates), and cars. Just make sure that the items are identical.

In addition you'll need objects that are similar, but not identical, such as three different baby shoes, different makes of cars, or a plastic spoon and a metal spoon. Put each of the identical objects in one bin and the dissimilar objects in another bin.

A large white rolling bin is a great investment for organizing materials. You should also obtain a few large recipe boxes to keep your child's pictures for his Verbal Behavior program.

To assess matching skills, lay three or four items on the floor or the table. (We call this a field of three or four.) The objects need a bit of space between them, so that the child may place the identical item next to its match. Hand the child a cup and say "Match." It is all right to give a small prompt in the beginning, so he'll know what is expected of him in this test. If the child matches all or most of the times in a field of four or five, you can begin to add in some items from the non-identical bin.

However, if your child begins to play with the toys on the table, or swats at them, or removes them from the table, then that is your starting point for this skill.

This same process can be used for matching pictures, too. One of the easiest ways to get matching pictures is to simply purchase two identical boxes of flashcards, as cheaply as possible. I've gotten some of the best materials over the years at discount and dollar stores. Flashcards can be used for a matching program as well as several other programs, so it's a good idea to have them at hand when you're beginning your program.

You can also purchase your supplies thorough websites including www.difflearn.com or www.superduperinc.com. It's also easy to use the internet to google particular items (under the images tab) and then print out two copies. This is a particularly good way to find more obscure objects such as fruit roll-ups or the White House. It's also very useful for picture to object matching.

If your child has excelled at both identical and non-identical matching of objects and pictures, the next step is to assess the child's ability to sort non-identical items. In this assessment you'd place pictures of different types of apples and different types of dogs on the table and ask the child to sort out all of the dogs. You can work on more complicated sorts, too, as the child succeeds, asking him to separate drinks versus animals, or vehicles versus foods.

Other visual performance skills include puzzle building, block design and maze completion.

Now that you have assessed the child in all areas, it's time to begin building on those skills to help your child learn.

CHAPTER 4

Developing Reinforcers

We All Respond to Positive Reinforcement

We all remember the high praise we've gotten in our lives. The applause at the grammar school play, the positive performance review, or the picture in the paper for catching the largest fish. And you probably discovered that once you received this praise, you wanted to continue to do things that would get you more praise. You wanted to perform better, work better, or fish better. Simply put, the rewards of your actions reinforced your determination and made your good behavior increase in the future.

Everyone responds to reinforcement, whether it is the obvious and dramatic applause for a job well done, or simply a paycheck at the end of a work week. We work because we get paid. We are polite to get a smile from a customer. We volunteer because we feel good helping others.

Children—even developmentally delayed children—are no different. When they are rewarded for behaviors they will respond positively. These rewards are called reinforcers and they are probably the most powerful tool that you'll have in helping your child with autism to learn. It's imperative that you identify powerful reinforcement for your child from the start.

Identifying Powerful Reinforcers

Please also remember that reinforcement needs to be individually applied to each child and is subject to change daily, so your list of reinforcers needs to be varied and broad. Some children love candy, but others hate it. Some will respond well to stickers or a token system with a somewhat delayed reinforcement, while others respond best to immediate reinforcement. Or, as I've said before, some children may find scolding and time outs to be reinforcing.

I had the wonderful opportunity to see Dr. Glen Latham speak in 2000, a few years before his death. Dr. Latham, author of *Power of Positive Parenting* (1990) among other books, stated that all humans need eight positives for every negative or constructive piece of feedback. Hearing his lecture was a life-changing event for me. He described classrooms that gave a lot of negative feedback and contrasted those with "good" classrooms where they learned to give eight positives to every negative. The positive things you do, however, can be nonverbal as well as verbal. Giving a child a thumbs up or even a smile can serve as reinforcement. I believe if all people in work and learning environments used this principle, adults and children would be much happier and productive. What I've learned over the years is that, if positive attention is not given abundantly enough, both children and adults will start acting out and displaying problem behaviors to get your negative attention. Another important thing I learned is that most children with developmental disabilities need a lot more than praise and a prize at the end of the week to comply and learn.

Developing a reinforcement system sounds like it would be simple, doesn't it? But actually, it's one of the harder things to do. Here's why: Children will respond to different reinforcers for different things at different times, based on the principles of satiation and deprivation.

No matter how much your child loves pretzels, he will not see them as a reinforcer once he has had his fill of them. Pretzels will no longer be a strong motivator. Imagine a child in a candy store—eventually he's going to have his fill of candy. Depriving a child of his favorite reinforcers may work sometimes, but there is a precarious balance here, too. While this may increase the value of the reinforcement, it may also create an atmosphere where the child believes he has to work too hard to watch just a few minutes of a favorite show. If the work is too hard in relation to the reinforcer, a child may decide it's not worth it. Children also go through phases where they love a particular food or activity or book, but then they stop liking it. This is true of typical children, too.

It's a complicated dance that you really end up creating as you go along. It's easy to begin, though, so that's where we'll start.

Choosing Reinforcers

When beginning a Verbal Behavior program you want to pick reinforcers that the instructor can easily control. For instance, a favorite toy would not be a good reinforcer in the beginning because there would be a tug of war at the end of the reinforcement period. Cookies, on the other hand, can be broken into tiny bits and doled out one at a time. Other easy-to-control reinforcers include one M&M candy, or a sip of juice poured from a big cup into a small cup. Once the candy or drink is consumed, the child can begin to work again, so he will get more of the juice or candy.

Food is often one of the best reinforcers, but parents and professionals alike balk at the idea of feeding a child all day with tiny bits of food. For some it smacks of dog training and for others there are issues about rewarding a child for such a small task. In addition, children with autism often have feeding disorders and are either underweight or overweight. They also tend to be extremely picky.

I worry about feeding children continuously through the day, too. I worry not only about their weight but also about their teeth if they're given sticky candy all day. Yet in my work I have met few children who didn't respond positively to edible reinforcement and I've seen only a few out of hundreds who respond to praise only in the beginning, so edibles almost always are used when setting up a VB program. The plan is, though, to keep the sips and the bites small, so that they don't add up to too much food. You can also try water or watered-down juice as the reinforcing liquid of choice. Favorite drinks as well as candy, pretzels, and Goldfish crackers often become the first items your child will be taught to mand for.

Using Videos and DVDs as Reinforcers

There are some non-edible, easily controlled reinforcers that you will need to use to help your child as well. One of the most powerful in that category is the use of television. Most children like to view videos or DVDs on a small or portable television. Now, you may be thinking, first I need to feed my child the food he prefers all day long and then I must let him watch television? When does he learn anything? Here again, you need to remember that this program is based on principles that work, that will allow your child to learn. Right now you are just figuring out the best reward system to help your child in the long run. As with the food reinforcers, television or video watching is permitted in small doses. A couple of minutes of productive work will lead to a child being able to watch his favorite video for 30 seconds. It's a good idea to purchase a small television that can be put on the work table, with a VHS and/or DVD built in. If that's not an option, set up the television as near to the work table as possible. Either way, you will need a remote control so that you can turn the television on and off quickly.

You may also be worried that your child will get upset once his favorite video is turned off (especially if it's his favorite part) or that he will want to eat more food than just the little bit that you offered. We'll learn later in the book how to best proceed with reinforcement during work, but right now let's begin by identifying what it is that will make your child respond.

The best way to do this is to watch your child watching a video. Does your child like the previews of the videos or the credits at the end? Does he have portions of videos that he plays over and over again? Write down the specifics of what your child enjoys most.

Examining Self-Stimulatory or Problem Behaviors to Develop Reinforcers

Finally, when determining your child's most powerful reinforcers, you'll need to look at your child's self-stimulatory behavior or any problem behavior to identify things that might be reinforcing. If your child grabs markers and colors on the walls and tables, consider using paper and crayons or a Magna Doodle as a reinforcer. If your child flicks his fingers in front of his eyes frequently, he is probably seeking additional visual stimulation. In these cases your child might find a spinning light-up toy reinforcing. Children who like to spin themselves until they are dizzy and fall down would likely respond to a sit-and-spin toy.

Completing a Reinforcer Assessment

Now it's time to get out a piece of paper and make a few categories of potential reinforcers. List all of the foods and drinks that your child enjoys. Then write a column that includes all of the videos and audio tapes that your child likes, including his favorite portions of the videos. Then you'll need to list a set of short reinforcers that can be supplied at the table. This list could include bubbles, a light-up spinning top, or a new duster that you can use to tickle your child. In a fourth column list activities away from the table that include movement. These might be bouncing the child on an exercise ball, rolling an exercise ball on top of the child, pushing the child on a swing, rolling the child in a blanket like a hot dog and then quickly unrolling him, balancing the child on your knees, dipping them upside down, or rocking the child very quickly in a chair.

For some children it will be necessary for you to fill out a reinforcement survey, observations, and assessments. If the person working with the child the most is not a caregiver, the parents should fill out a short reinforcer survey (different reinforcer surveys are available from www.establishingoperation-sinc.com or www.verbalbehaviornetwork.com). Professionals may also have to observe the child prior to creating a program. This really can be as simple as handing a child an M&M candy and seeing if he takes it. Or giving the child a bowl of chips and recording how long it takes him to eat it.

While you are making your notes, it's important to be specific, as children with autism are quite brand loyal and picky. Lucas only likes drinking milk contained in a small carton with a straw, and will only eat Cheerios out of a bowl. He would not be reinforced if I handed him one Cheerio or if I gave him a Dixie cup with a sip-full of water or milk. If a teacher reports to you that a reinforcer is not working at school, check to make sure that it's delivered in the way your child prefers. In general, if multiple people are working with your child (which is likely) you'll need to be very detailed in describing reinforcers.

If ever your child cries, screams, or pushes a reinforcer away, you'll need to double check to make sure that the reinforcer is the appropriate object delivered in the correct way.

Another way to complete a reinforcer assessment is to lay out potential reinforcers on the work table and see which the child selects and how long he plays with it or (in the case of edibles) consumes first. Still another option is to put many different toys, activities, and foods in a room or on a table and then observe the child's interactions with them. You can record the child's preferences without any involvement from you and also when you are present. For instance, if Katie is swinging and appears happy, and you approach her and give her a push, record her reaction. Does your involvement make the activity more or less fun for

Katie? If Bobby is looking at a book and you begin to narrate a few things in the book, is the activity better or worse for Bobby? Is it reinforcing for him to just flip through the pages randomly, or reinforcing to have you interact with him? If he likes the book alone at this point, that is where you start.

However, for all reinforcers, eventually you'll want to pair the adult with the reinforcement and have the child like to hear the adult narrate. We want people (not just snacks, toys, and activities) to become conditioned reinforcers for the child so we can use praise and more natural reinforcers in addition to snacks and movies.

When you are done making all your lists, you can rank the reinforcers according to their usefulness.

Once you know your child's reinforcers it really is best to begin with something small and controllable. This might be something that is consumed or that disappears after use. A piece of candy that is eaten, or a blow on a bubble wand where the bubbles dissipate quickly, are two good examples of controllable reinforcers.

If this isn't possible—some children are best reinforced with things they can hold or manipulate like a book or string—be very gentle when retrieving the reinforcer. In the beginning you may have to trade a piece of candy to get a book back, or you may have to allow a child to have several reinforcers at a time. It is imperative that the child see the instructor or parent as the giver of all things not a taker. Eventually—early in your program—the child will learn to give up the reinforcer without a struggle if the adult carefully gets the item back without grabbing.

If you're having trouble finding reinforcers that work for your child, don't despair. It's just tougher with some children who don't seem to get excited about anything. But I believe that all children and adults, no matter what their level of functioning, will be motivated by something. So it may turn out that self-stimulatory behavior will be a reinforcer in the beginning of your program. If the only thing that motivates your child is spinning or flapping his hands, that needs to be used to develop a reinforcer. This self-stimulatory behavior will be the starting point but you need to develop a reinforcer that is similar to this but that you can control. The goal is to find something more appealing than their hands or fingers that you can deliver.

Developing Age-Appropriate Reinforcers

As you can see, I don't really think that there are many taboo reinforcers. I often get questions from parents about their children's likes. What if my ten-year-old finds *Teletubbies* to be the most reinforcing video? What if my five-year-old likes to play with a baby toy made for an 18-month-old? I say, don't panic. First, look at your child's developmental age, not just his chronological age. If a ten-year-old has the language skills of a two-year-old it's not surprising that he wants to watch *Teletubbies*. That show is appropriate for his skills. Watching *Teletubbies* is a starting reinforcer and you can gently guide the child towards more age-appropriate reinforcers as he gains skills and confidence. Start with *Teletubbies* and then try to add in *Sesame Street*. Eventually you can move away from *Sesame Street*, too, and work on adding videos like *Arthur* or *Sponge Bob Squarepants*.

I also don't think you can have too many reinforcers. Trust me, you will continue to increase the number and type of reinforcers. If you remember about the rules of satiation and deprivation, it won't be surprising to learn that your child will simply get his fill of a particular reinforcer, especially if you don't limit access to those items.

Which brings up the next point. Once you have identified your child's reinforcers, make sure that he doesn't have unlimited access to them. Before we started using the Verbal Behavior approach in our home we commonly had reinforcers strewn around the floor of the therapy room. Since we used the Lovaas approach for one year, our therapist would take breaks in teaching and tell Lucas to "go play." Lucas would look around the room and might select a toy to play with for a minute or two before he was called back to the table. In a VB program, the child's reinforcers are kept in clear bins, baggies, or high up on shelves. The child should be unable to gain access to the reinforcers without the help of an adult. This forces some communication between child and adult, where the child needs the adult and, we hope, will begin to think of them as the giver of all good things.

Pairing the Learning Environment with Reinforcement

The process called "pairing" is the next step in the program. Pairing is actually the process of pairing the environment, people, and materials with the child's already established reinforcers. You should have already identified your child's reinforcers and placed them out of the child's reach in the work area, so that you can control them. Pairing is an ongoing process and is not something that can be done in a few days or a week. I've actually heard professionals say, "We are going to pair for one week, and then we are going to get to work."

This is not effective.

Pairing needs to be reinforced throughout the time any caregiver or professional works with the child, although it is paramount in a school or therapy session where the demands are quite high.

It's important to remember that even if you are a parent, as you work through the VB approach, you'll find that you do become one of your child's teachers and therapists. In fact, right now is a good time to consider creating a therapy space in your home. It can be as small as a child's table in the corner of a room, or it can be an entire room or basement. It's just going to be the place where the child works and you have the materials available to teach your child. Pairing this area with reinforcement is key.

What you're looking for in your therapy area is a place where the child will want to go. You'll want him to be running to the table to do the work. You'll want him to eventually be excited about seeing the flash-cards and other materials for learning and be happy to use them. You'll want a child who exhibits no problem behaviors during the sessions. Sound like a fantasy?

It's not. The goal of any academic program is that the child is a happy and willing learner. That's what you're looking for in your home program, too. You want a child who wants to be there.

Just as there are ways to tell if you're creating that type of environment, there are also things that indicate that it's not working. If, for instance, your child cries and flees outside when the therapist rings your doorbell, you'll need to reassess how the therapist is perceived. Or if your child protests going to school at all, this signals that the school environment has not been paired with reinforcement. In those cases you'll have to start again by finding ways to pair the teacher and the environment with reinforcement.

How to Pair with Reinforcement

Once you have identified your reinforcers, you'll need to find ways to associate yourself (or whomever is working with your child) as well as the room and materials with these items of interest. This is called "pairing" and the process is simple and fun. The adult should have several of the child's strong reinforcers readily available and should go towards the child and give them the reinforcers without placing any demands on the child. At first—if your child has an aversion to a teacher or therapist—the child may not take the reinforcer from the adult's hand. In this case the adult needs to begin by laying a chip next to the child, or by turning on the television set and then leaving the table. This way, the child feeds himself the chip or watches the television alone. The teacher then works incrementally towards the goal of having the child take the reinforcer in their presence. Some children require more work in this area than others. Don't take it personally. It just means that you'll have to work harder and more slowly to gain the child's trust.

If your child will take a reinforcer from you, begin by just handing the child the item, remaining silent. Once he is taking the item from you quickly without a problem, you begin to pair your voice with the presentation of the item, by labeling it. When you are delivering the reinforcer say, "Chip, chip…here Jimmy, a chip."

Continue on this way until the child is tolerant of you approaching him and offering the item. Once that comfort level is met, the next step is to place the reinforcers on the work table, a short distance away from the child, and see if the child will approach you. This could be as close as reaching towards the item from his seat. Once he begins his approach, deliver the reinforcer without demanding anything. At this point, the child doesn't need to say or sign anything.

As time passes, the therapist can move the items further and further from the child, so that the child needs to eventually get up from what he is doing and take a few steps towards the therapist. You might want to invest in a tool apron with pockets so that you can carry reinforcers on your body at all times. This way the child learns that the adult working with him has access to all the things he loves and will hand them over often without requiring any work.

The use of reinforcers and pairing the teacher with them is the essential first step of a Verbal Behavior program. It makes sense that a child would need to approach a teacher eagerly to be ready to learn. At this beginning point in the program it's too early, really, to put demands on the child. If you're having difficult with pairing, you'll probably need to reassess the reinforcers that you're using, and make sure the environment itself is paired with reinforcement.

Some children—about half that I've worked with—are very easy to pair with, and the work can begin relatively quickly. Once the child approaches you or the teacher or the therapist, and appears happy, it's time for the teacher to begin to interact with the child. You can begin by narrating what's on the television or tickle the child, bounce him on your knee, or sing songs. Pairing less-preferred items or activities with strong reinforcers is also important. So, if Katie loves the swing but doesn't seem to particularly like when people sing, pairing these two activities actually can condition the singing to become more preferred in the future.

Easing in Demands

If you've discovered that your child is easy to pair with, remember to keep the demands very low in the beginning. The biggest mistake I see people make when working with "easy-to-pair-with" children is that they move onto demands too quickly. When work begins—and it should begin once a child is happily approaching the work area—it's important that the child does not really know that he is working. If the child notices the transition between pure reinforcement and work, then it's too drastic.

How will you know when it's time to begin work? You'll need to observe your child's behavior as you begin to slowly introduce demands. Before any demands are made, the child should be coming to the work area and sitting nicely for at least a few minutes. The child should be able to tolerate your (or the therapist's) voice, as well as light touches to his arms and back.

The first place to start is by asking the child to learn to say or sign their desire for a particular reinforcer. Begin with your child's absolute favorite item.

This will lay the groundwork for manding, which you'll begin working on, once the environment is adequately paired with reinforcement. You might also slip in some work with imitation by using toys, matching identical objects, and putting simple puzzles together. You can refer to the results of your Verbal Behavior assessment to come up with some demands that will be extremely easy for your child to complete.

The purpose of these activities is to show him how easy it is to get reinforcement, making him eager to learn.

The VR Schedule of Reinforcement

As you work at pairing reinforcement and making small demands, you'll need to be aware of the variable ratio schedule of reinforcement (VR). The VR is the average number of correct responses displayed by the child in between reinforcements. In the beginning you will be offering reinforcement with no demands. Then you will gradually begin to increase your demands, giving reinforcement after every correct response. That is called "continuous reinforcement ratio." Then you'll implement a VR schedule.

Unlike a fixed schedule of reinforcement, a VR schedule is useful because a child doesn't know when the reinforcement is coming, although there will only be a few demands before a strong reinforcer is presented. This type of schedule has been shown to produce a strong, steady response over time.

A VR schedule is planned by the adult and is increased incrementally over time. A VR of two means that a child might be required to perform one, two, three, or four tasks before reinforcement, as long as the average number of responses during a work session equaled two. Each set of tasks is called a "run-through," a term coined by Holly Kibbe and Cherish Twiggs (2001). The first run-through using a VR of two might be three prior to reinforcement and then the next run-through would include only one demand before reinforcement.

For instance, if the child is on a VR of three, you may have one run through of activities where the child performs four tasks before reinforcement, while the next run-through has only two tasks. That would average out to the number three.

Here are examples of a work run-through with a VR of three.

Give the child a chip before you begin to work, as reinforcement. Then, say "Touch your nose"—the child complies (response one). Point to a cup and say "What's this?"—the child responds appropriately (response two). Point to a photo of a dog and say "What's this?"—the child complies by saying "dog" (response three). Say "Stand up"—the child stands up (response four). Then say, "Let's go jump on the trampoline," which is a strong reinforcer for the child. In this case the number of responses for the run-through (the course of correct responses between reinforcement) was four.

The child goes on the trampoline with the instructor holding the child's hands and bounces the child (reinforcement). Then the instructor starts the next run-through and sings, "Ten little monkeys jumping on the…" and the child fills in "bed," (response one). The adult stops the child on the trampoline and says "jump" (response two); and then the child gets the reinforcement of jumping. The number of responses for this run-through is two. When the two sample run-throughs are averaged together, the VR for this child is three.

Increasing the VR schedule should be done slowly and carefully and should be adjusted based on a child's performance. If the child is having some escape issues at the work table, you'll need to lower your VR before the session starts. Some children require a lower VR on Mondays or whenever they've had a break from schooling. If the child is not cooperative at the table, whether he is displaying aggression, self-injurious behavior, or using self-stimulatory behavior, the VR is almost always way too high. Backing up to pure pairing might be necessary. Oftentimes taking a big step backward and then being more careful when raising demands will pay off in the long run.

As with all parts of the VB approach, everyone working with the child must be aware of, and implement the same VR schedule. Also remember that good work does need to be rewarded and if a child is working well at a task, he should *not* be penalized by an increased VR during that session. The VR should be gradually increased over days or weeks, not during one session.

Keeping track of the VR will help you gauge when your child works best and is a particularly good way to treat problem behaviors at the work table. Parents and professionals alike don't always realize when they are putting too many demands on a child. Problem behavior during intensive teaching is almost always an indicator of this. Adults may think that they are engaging a child and playing with him, when in fact, their play is full of demands with no reinforcement. A VR schedule keeps adults on task because it makes them aware of the demands they are making on their child.

This chapter has shown you ways to define and use reinforcement to help your child to learn. Reinforcement is so essential to the Verbal Behavior approach, that if you cannot get your child's school teacher, therapist, or consultant to buy into the fact that your child needs more than an occasional "Good job" during the day, your program will fail.

I have found that some teachers balk at the idea of using edibles or television in the classroom as reinforcement. But remember, it's not the adults who pick the reinforcement, it's the children. Yet teachers complain that the toys or videos will be disruptive to the other children, and that it's not fair for only one child to be given candy throughout the day. Unfortunately, it's impossible for a Verbal Behavior program to proceed without everyone understanding and embracing the concept of reinforcement. Work with your child's teacher and caregivers as much as necessary to help them to understand how essential these items are to your child's academic and personal growth.

A powerful, individualized reinforcement system is imperative for any school or home-based Verbal Behavior program. And once it's in place, it's time to begin the real work of this program: Teaching your child to communicate with you.

CHAPTER 5

Manding

When Lucas was two years old he wasn't talking much and was diagnosed with a language delay. He immediately began speech therapy. Even though I didn't know that he had autism, I still wanted him to have the best opportunities available—and I wanted to help him as much as possible.

I attended his weekly speech sessions and it wasn't long before I was asking his speech pathologist for tools that I could use at home to help him. To my surprise she couldn't recommend one single book, but encouraged me to watch what she did in the sessions and then replicate it at home. I couldn't imagine that there were no resources for parents so I did some investigation and found *It Takes Two to Talk*, which explains the Hanen Method (Manolson 1992).

To be honest, at this point I wasn't looking for a book that described how to help children with autism speak, as I was still very much in denial about the potential for that diagnosis. If you are reading this book and your child has a language delay but has not yet been diagnosed with autism (and may never be) I applaud your courage in reading all books that might help your child. These particular interventions will help language development in typical babies as well. A friend of mine suggested that I include autism treatments for my son when he was diagnosed with a speech delay, but I didn't listen because I was afraid of the possibility of autism. In fact, had Lucas only had a language delay, the Applied Behavior Analysis (ABA) treatment for autism would have helped him more than speech therapy alone.

Some of the suggestions in *It Takes Two to Talk* included placing items on high shelves, sabotaging routines, and labeling single words over and over again. Those techniques worked like magic for Lucas, who more than doubled his vocabulary and began to request items more frequently. Lucas's speech therapist did have a broad enough background to know that when children are taught to request things, they learn faster and behave better. But we had no idea about pairing the environment with reinforcement or easing demands in gradually. In fact I didn't even know what a VR (variable ratio schedule of reinforcement) was until Lucas was six years old—more than four years after he started speech therapy.

During the speech sessions, the therapist would start with a fun activity, such as blowing bubbles, and then would attempt to get Lucas to ask for more bubbles. That was her way of teaching him to mand—to make a demand or a request. This was a successful strategy, but then she'd move quickly to turn taking and abstract concepts such as answering yes or no to a question, or using prepositions and pronouns and plurals. Lucas was happy with the bubbles and the manding, but once the sessions went beyond that, his behavior went downhill quickly.

Manding is integral to the Verbal Behavior (VB) approach. It's based on having a need met and, as reported earlier in this book, it is predicated on motivation. A child must be motivated to ask for something, either by hunger or by desire of another sort. The child has a desire for juice, mands for it, and receives it. Manding has an immediate positive benefit since during this therapy, a mand is always immediately reinforced—the item or activity is immediately delivered.

Problem behaviors, according to Dr. Mark Sundberg and other experts in VB, are almost always caused by a mand defect—an inability to make your needs known. This is true across the board. Show me a toddler—or even an adult—with a behavior problem and I'll show you someone who hasn't learned to effectively mand for items, actions, or information they want.

Vocal language is not the only way to get needs met. Babies use crying to such perfection that many parents say they can tell the difference between a cry for food or a cry for a diaper change. I was never good at that skill, but did realize that if one of my sons was crying, they needed something. Crying is a newborn's first mand and an essential skill for survival. As infants grow, their demands become more specific and their manding skills need to keep up. A six- or eight-month-old infant wants to be picked up, or wants juice instead of milk, and will somehow develop a communication system to get those newer needs met. A typical child will learn to point or to hold out arms or employ some other gesture. A child with autism or other developmental delay may not develop those gesturing skills and this is, in fact, a hallmark symptom for autism: Failure to point by 18 months of age. Crying will likely continue instead and thus begins a pattern of crying and tantrumming in a child who cannot communicate his needs.

Teaching a child to mand is an essential skill if your child is to ever learn to communicate with you, so be sure you are armed with very strong reinforcers and a work area that is paired with reinforcement before you begin. Re-read Chapter 4 if you need directions about how to do this. You'll also need to know that your child is motivated for some things. This is usually indicated by his reaching for an item on the table (such as a cookie or juice) or taking you by the hand and leading you to an item or an activity. Some children will point out their desires or use non-specific vocalizations to indicate their desire for something.

Let's use the example of Timmy, a four-year-old child, recently diagnosed with autism. His parents are anxious to begin an ABA/VB program. Timmy can say a few words, but does not mand for anything, even if items he wants are in view. Since manding for items that are in view is easier than manding for actions or items that are out of sight, we'll focus on teaching Timmy to vocally mand for items that are in sight. (Different strategies for non-vocal children will be outlined in the next chapter.)

Timmy is able to tact (label) items, including ball, book, bed, and airplane. Timmy's favorite reinforcers are chips, candy, juice, water, Barney books and videos, swinging on a swing, jumping on a small trampoline, and bouncing on a large exercise ball. His parents have purchased a small child-sized table, placed it in the family room near the television, and hired a therapist with a small amount of experience under her belt to work with him three times a week. Timmy has shown little interest in sitting at the table and resists going to it, if directed by his therapist or his mother. He will complete puzzles on the floor and likes to line up and match cars, but he doesn't like it when an adult tries to intervene when he's playing. Both his mother and his therapist believe they are ready to begin teaching him to mand. Right?

Wrong!

Here are some issues in this case that need to be addressed prior to beginning to teach manding. First and foremost, the environment is not paired enough with reinforcement for the program to succeed. Rushing into the program is really one of the most common mistakes that I see when professionals and parents try to set up VB programs. If you rush into demands, your child will not react well to what is occurring. It's so prevalent a problem that I see it in nearly every home and school consultation that I do.

You cannot have too much reinforcement in the environment.

Before you begin to make even one demand on your child, you'll need to make sure that he is running to the therapist and is happy to be near people on the floor or at the table. He should be reaching for preferred items and taking the reinforcers that are given to him without any demand made. This is when you'll want to start your mand training.

To begin, take a good look at the words that Timmy is already saying and analyze them to see which might make good first mands. Since Timmy can tact (label) ball and book, and two of his reinforcers are bouncing on a ball and looking at Barney books, those two mands should be among the first you teach. Most early learners should learn three to five mands in the beginning. Since Timmy can already say a few words, I'd start with five mands in his case.

Don't focus on only one mand at a time, as it will become over-generalized. For instance if your child learns to mand "movie" and gets to watch a bit of a movie after each mand for movie, he will eventually learn that whenever he wants to watch the movie, he needs to say "movie." But, if this child is only taught one mand, he might also over-generalize the use of this by requesting "movie" when he wants other things such as juice or ball. This is why it is essential you teach three to five mands at a time.

Another error that some make when teaching children to mand, is using words like "more" and "please." These are words that are often taught early by people inexperienced in an ABA/VB approach. Children learn that if they want something, they can mand "more" and it will be delivered. But they are not learning the actual mand for an item. Words like "please" and "more" are abstract concepts that a language-impaired child will likely not understand. Instead you want to teach a child to mand for an actual item *in* sight, that will eventually be phased *out* of sight in the hope that your child will be able to mand, for example, for ice cream, when it is in the freezer. That will never happen, if Timmy is learning "more", since the ice cream will be out of sight and the adult will have no idea what Timmy wants "more" of.

In addition, you don't want to ask a language-delayed child to request items using full sentences. If your child wants a cookie and mands "cookie," it's appropriate to deliver the cookie. Improvement should not be measured by how long your child's sentences are, but rather how many different needs and wants he is able to communicate using words or signs. Combining words should come after your child is fairly fluent in asking for many items that are out of sight. Once that is accomplished, you can begin to work on two- or three-word phrases that help to identify an item, such as a red skittle or a chocolate chip cookie or a sugar cookie. Words will be added one at a time, and they should add meaning to the phrase to help the child further specify his needs.

Now that you know what not to do, you're ready to begin teaching Timmy to mand.

You've selected a few target mands, including ball and book. Since you already know that Timmy can say the words, and they are reinforcers for him, it should be easy to teach him to mand for them. It's important to keep tasks easy in the beginning.

In addition to ball and book, you'll need to pick two food items. As a rule of thumb, it's a good idea to pick a couple of food items and a couple of activities as the first mands. Don't pick five food items, because you should teach manding throughout the day as your child wants to engage in different activities. If all of your initial mands are food items, you will only be able to teach manding at snack time.

Look again at Timmy's reinforcer list and consider how available his edible reinforcers are. Difficult items for first mands would be things like french fries or bacon or ice cream, which would be difficult to deliver throughout the day because they would need to be kept warm, or cold. Since candy and chips are listed on his reinforcer list, and they are easy to deliver, I'd pick those items. I'd add juice as the fifth item, since he appears to prefer it to water.

When deciding which mands to choose in the beginning, imagine that you are in a foreign country where you don't know the language. What are the first words that you would want to learn, so that you can have your needs met? You would want to learn to ask for the bathroom, water, pizza, food, a taxi, a train, or a hotel. The same is true for your child who needs to learn the best words to have his needs met.

So these are the five mands we're targeting: ball, book, chips, candy, and juice. These are the first words we'll teach Timmy to use to request items.

Here you'll need to keep in mind that while a typical child will learn to mand after just a few trials, it may take a developmentally delayed child hundreds or thousands of trials to learn to request. It's your job to make sure that he has many chances to do this throughout the day. In fact you'll be aiming to give your child hundreds of opportunities per day to mand. This means you will have to create an atmosphere where your child will be motivated to request things over and over again.

Manding should occur throughout the day, but it's also important to set aside several mand sessions throughout the day. To do a mand session you'll need to take one of the reinforcers (chips, for example) and divide it into small pieces. Ten chips can be broken into four pieces each, and one cookie into ten pieces, and you'll be able to set up a mand session where your child gets a total of 50 opportunities to mand for two items that he loves. A manding session can take as little as two minutes, or as long as a half-hour to complete. This is time where you are completely focused on getting your child to mand, and the session will also allow you to do more positive pairing with your child.

To prepare for a mand session, you'll need to gather the five reinforcers and choose where the session will take place. This can be on the floor or at the work table, whichever the child prefers. Put the chips and the candy in clear baggies, so that the child can see them. Place a small cup on the table, in addition to a container of juice. This will allow you to pour and deliver small sips of juice to Timmy.

If you've chosen strong reinforcers and paired the work area with reinforcement, your child should approach you when he sees five of his favorite things laid out in front of you. He will likely indicate which one he wants first. He may begin to bounce on the ball, or to grab the bag of chips. Since you cannot make a child speak, you'll have to use a "back door" method to get Timmy to mand. Timmy will probably join the mand session voluntarily because he sees his strongest reinforcers are available and might begin bouncing on a ball. You should grasp his hands and begin to bounce him higher, since you know that he likes this. After he's clearly having fun bouncing on the ball (and he's encouraging you to continue, not pushing you away) say the word "ball" three times, very clearly. Wait one or two seconds between each word.

Don't worry that he's bouncing on the ball, and that he may confuse the word "bouncing" with the word "ball." You are relying on the fact that Timmy can already say the word "ball," and that is your starting point. After your child has been happily bouncing on the ball for a minute or so, use your hands, which are already touching Timmy's hands, to slow him down enough so that he stops bouncing. Now that the reinforcement has stopped, you'll want to quickly pair the word "ball" (three times) once again. And then begin bouncing him.

If at any time during this session Timmy echoes you or says the word "ball" spontaneously, you need to immediately bounce him vigorously, lavishing him with praise, and reinforcers, while you say, "Good saying ball!" "Ball, ball...Timmy said ball," or other similar phrases.

It's important to keep the demands very light and very simple in the beginning. Don't use phrases such as: "If you want to bounce on the ball, you've got to say BALL...say BALL." This is a huge demand, although it may not seem that way to you. To Timmy it's nearly impossible to process and will clearly indicate that the reinforcement has stopped and the work has begun. For the time being, Timmy's mand sessions will look very much like advanced pairing sessions where the instructor will pair the item's name two or three times, when delivering the reinforcement.

Timmy may not vocalize ball at all during the mand session and that's fine. Stick with it until Timmy loses interest in the ball or you want to move onto a different mand. For some children who have one reinforcer that is a strong favorite (a ten on a scale of one to ten) it might be necessary to remove that reinforcer from the work area if you want to move onto another item. Mand sessions should also be conducted when Timmy is hungry, so that he will be motivated to request the edibles you have for him.

Here's a strategy for mixing up the reinforcers during a mand session when one reinforcer is a clear favorite: Give Timmy a chip and label the item three times while he is sitting still on the ball and then move the ball closer to the table, so he doesn't have to get off of it to work with other items. In this case the ball will serve as Timmy's chair while he's learning. Whatever you do, don't drag him off the ball and over to the table, as this will negate all of the pairing that you've done. If he is truly motivated for the ball and not for his other targeted mands, you cannot work on the other items. As I stated previously, the mand must always be preceded by motivation.

Continue a similar process with the other items. When teaching Timmy to mand for his Barney book, simply work on the word "book." Once Timmy has acquired several mands, you can move him up to two-word pivotal phrases such as "bounce ball," or "roll ball," or "Barney book" versus "Spot Book."

Once Timmy has spontaneously manded for one of his target items, you may add an additional target to your list. When selecting additional targets make sure to continue to mix up the types of mands between edibles, items, and activities and pick one word as the target response for each mand.

But what if it doesn't work? What if you've done hundreds of trials with his favorite reinforcers and Timmy still isn't manding? It does happen, but there is a strategy. You'll need to begin to pair words with sign language; this is extensively covered in the next chapter. Don't worry that your child will never speak. Sign language is a strategy that can easily be prompted and sometimes it's all a child needs to make the connection between the word and the request.

The good news is in most cases with children like Timmy who can vocally say some words, careful pairing and frequent mand sessions do result in manding for items. Once he has several dozen words he can mand for in sight, you'll begin to work on manding for items that are out of sight. The best way to start work on that is to select actions that are always out of sight. "Push" on a swing, for example. Or "tickle," "open," or "move" work well, too. When fading actual items out of sight, just make sure to do it very gradually by first giving Timmy a chip and getting him to request it a few times. Once he's done that a few times, but still wants more, you can move the bag under the table or put it behind something on the table. If Timmy doesn't request it once it's out of sight, you can flash it at him quickly, or verbally prompt him, and then deliver the chip.

How do you know if you're making progress with Timmy? It's important to collect data, so that you'll know how much he is learning. This is great for him, but also for you. Sometimes it may feel like you're not getting far, but you will be able to access your data and know really how far you and Timmy have come.

Data collection is very important to all areas of the Verbal Behavior approach, and you will be very glad you did it, as the program progresses and becomes more sophisticated. You can use the same clicker counter that you used to track problem behavior to help you track positive progress. You can buy a few clicker counters at just about any office supply store, or www.difflearn.com. You'll want to have a couple around for the different programs throughout the day. Everyone should collect data during mand sessions by clicking one counter each time the child produces a mand. You can write down the number of mands obtained next to the time spent manding. Then, clear the counter number back to "0" to prepare for the next session.

Once you get the hang of counting mands, you can also use two clickers at the same time during mand sessions and keep track of prompted mands on one clicker (where you say chip and he echoes you) and independent mands on another (where he says chip without a verbal prompt). In the beginning you'll prompt for mands at least twice as often as the number of mands that are independent.

Another option instead of using clickers initially, is to simply make a tally sheet with the five targeted mands listed and then mark the word each time it's manded (see Table 5.1) This will help you to see if your child is manding for one item a lot and the others infrequently.

Table 5.1 Manding Tally Sheet		
Date: July 6th Time Manding: 15 minutes		
	Prompted	**Independent/item in sight**
Ball	I I I I I I I	I I I
Book	I I	I I I I I I I
Chip	I I I I I I I I I	I
Candy	I I	I I I I I I I
Juice	I I I I I I	I

Either way, you'll have information that lets you know if, and how, your program is working. If you're at all competitive, it will give you additional incentive to increase the number of mands each day or each week. Before you move on to higher-level manding you've got to make sure that the foundation of your child's language is strong. It may be years before your child is ready to mand for things like "attention" or "information," but he will be communicating with you long before that. Take heart in that, as this will be a lifelong process for you and your child.

However, once your child is ready to move onto the next step, you'll want to begin to teach your child more sophisticated concepts. Remember to go at his own pace so that reinforcement will remain high. Once your child is manding for many items and actions and activities both in and out of sight, you can move up to mands that include asking for attention. These include phrases such as, "Hey, watch this" or "Look what I did" or "Look, there's a cow." This is complex because, as we've learned earlier, there needs to be motivation for a word or a phrase to be a mand. Timmy needs to want your attention and then ask for it, for this to be a true mand. While it's fairly easy to create motivation for edibles, it's a lot more difficult to get your child to want you to look at a cow.

Another mand that your child will eventually learn, is manding for information. Manding for information includes requests such as, "Where are my shoes?" or "What's in the bag?" or "How did you do that?" Teaching these mands for information is also difficult, but it can be done. Remember again to go slowly. You'll need to work with reinforcers to entice the child to want to know some sort of information. For instance, you can place several of his favorite reinforcers into an opaque bag and then shake it to entice the child. When the child tries to peer in the bag to see what's inside (that would be the motivation) you'll need to prompt Timmy to say "What?" or "What's in the bag?" and then give him the information by giving him the bag and letting him extract his reinforcer.

There is extensive information on teaching the more complex mands at www.establishingoperationsinc.com, a great website developed by Holly Kibbe and Cherish Twiggs.

Once your child is manding to have his needs met, it's likely you'll see an improvement in his behavior. If you don't, you'll have to go back to your list and see if you've included things that he needs and wants and to make sure that your environment is as rich as possible. Your child will get there.

Now it's time to move onto other verbal operants that will enhance your child's communication skills. It may not sound like much so far, but I think you'll be happy when you see your child able to communicate even in one-word mands. It's quite likely music to your ears. Your child is talking to you! Let's keep the momentum going.

CHAPTER 6

Increasing and Improving Speech in Non-Vocal or Minimally Vocal Children

There will be times when you can do everything right, and still your child won't speak.

In Chapter 5 I described techniques that would allow you to begin teaching your child to mand using some spoken words.

Let's go back to Timmy from Chapter 5 and imagine that, even though you've heard him say a few words, he's not responding to the program and is not manding vocally, even with the item in sight and after you've provided a voice model three times for hundreds of trials.

There are some children who will not mand no matter how hard you work with them, or how high the reinforcement is. You'll notice fairly soon if this is the case with your child, and if it is, you'll need to move on to a different plan. You don't want to be giving constant reinforcement to a child who is not learning. The rules of reinforcement are that a behavior that is reinforced will increase—so if you are rewarding Timmy for not speaking or communicating in any way, then his silence will be reinforced.

It's confusing, I know, but there are systems available to help you help your child communicate, even if it's not vocally. Using a non-vocal program is the place you need to start if your child has never spoken, or if you have tried to get him to vocally mand and he has not.

It is impossible to force someone to talk, so prompting spoken words is useless. If you say "Say cat," to your child and he doesn't respond, there is no way that you can force the air through his vocal chords to make him create the word. You can, however, help him sign the word cat, or point to a picture of a cat. There are several effective strategies to increase the chances of getting your non-vocal child to speak. These strategies will also help children to communicate more clearly so that whatever vocal language they have will be enhanced.

Figuring out strategies to help non-vocal children become vocal has been a strong interest of mine since I became a Board Certified Behavior Analyst (BCBA) in 2003. I would often sit down to work with older children who—according to reports from parents and professionals alike—did not speak. Within minutes these children were making word approximations!

When I was in classrooms working with these children, the professionals observing would be amazed at the progress that was made, believing it to be some sort of magic. But all I was doing was implementing procedures that I learned from experts such as Dr. Mark Sundberg and Dr. Vincent Carbone. Procedures that you, too, can implement at home.

In my professional life I was able to try out these techniques on students at varying levels on the autism spectrum and even some other students who had been diagnosed with other disorders, including Down Syndrome.

Dr. Carbone's video examples are equally astonishing, and actually look too good to be true. But believe it. It is possible that your non-vocal child can talk. I've worked with students as old as 14 who have developed real, functional speech, within months of switching to a Verbal Behavior approach.

Speech therapy can be helpful, especially when used in a behavioral framework, but standard speech therapy often fails with children who are completely non-vocal. This is underlined by the good results gotten by speech pathologists Joanne Gerenser, Nancy Kaufman, and Tamara Kasper, who have incorporated an ABA-based approach into their techniques.

There are several techniques that are supported by research to increase a child's likelihood of producing or improving speech. Sign language is far and away my best strategy and my first choice for teaching non-vocal children to mand.

Sign Language Versus Other Augmentative Communication Systems

Augmentative communication systems include any systems used to augment or support language. ABA practitioners familiar with B.F. Skinner's analysis of Verbal Behavior most often recommend sign language.

Very few children that are introduced to a VB program are using an augmentative system that's working. In fact, even if they do have some sign language, I've found that they are often prompt-dependent or using general signs such as "please" and "more." When I come into the picture and see a child with no language and/or with an augmentative system that is clearly not working, I need to consider the slate clean to begin my work.

There are three types of augmentative systems that are most commonly used: sign language; voice output devices; and the Picture Exchange Communication System (PECS).

Whenever possible I choose sign language because it's portable, it's comprehensive for use in the VB approach across all the different operants of words, and research has shown that, when accompanied by spoken words, it works to improve vocalization.

If a child can sign, then I can work with him when he's in a pool or jumping on a trampoline, which could be two very high reinforcers. A child's hands are always available, making it possible for hundreds of opportunities to work on manding while the child is having lots of fun.

Sign language also shows children visually that words are different. The sound for "ball" and "cookie" are different, as are the signs. Similar to speech, there is a distinct movement for each word. So once the child learns to sign for cookie, it's usually pretty easy to teach them to sign "cookie" when he sees a picture, or to eventually answer questions with that same sign, such as, "Tell me something you eat." This enables the child to eventually use sign language across operants.

There are some disadvantages to sign language though. Adults must be trained to use it and for it to be effective all adults working with the child need to have an understanding of ABA principles such as pairing, reinforcement, prompting, shaping, and prompt fading. The other commonly cited disadvantage is that sign language is not universal in the community so those at McDonald's won't understand the sign for "hamburger." This does become an issue as the child ages, but if the child is still in preschool or elementary school with a significant language impairment, there is time to use sign language before the child will be out in the community alone. All family members, though, will need to learn the child's signs. This is best accomplished by the use of a homemade picture/sign dictionary that includes a picture and description of each of the child's signs or by videotaping a skilled professional demonstrating the child's mastered signs.

Voice Output Systems

A voice output system is a device where the child selects and pushes a button and the machine produces the speech. There are simple models where a child only needs to discriminate between a few preferred items all the way up to extremely sophisticated systems that require a child to have advanced receptive language skills and produce sentences.

To use these systems the adults working with the child would need to be fairly skilled at updating the system by downloading pictures and making sure the device is operational. The adult also needs to help the child troubleshoot if the device malfunctions or needs repair and the child would need a back-up system, if the voice output system was out for repair. These devices are somewhat cumbersome and do require a fair amount of receptive language ability too. Systems can also cost more than $5000, making this the most costly alternative.

Picture Exchange Communication System

This system, usually called PECS, is a systematic approach that involves teaching the child to use pictures to mand for items. I was trained in PECS by the developers of the system, Dr. Andy Bondy and Ms. Lori Frost, shortly after my son was enrolled in an ABA school which implemented PECS frequently, even for verbal students.

One advantage of both voice output systems as well as PECS is that words produced by voice output systems and pictures from PECS are easy for adults and other children to understand.

Although PECS is certainly more affordable than voice output devices, there are disadvantages here, too. After the initial stages of PECS, the child must learn to pick out some fairly abstract pictures to trade with an adult for an item. For instance, corn chips must be selected from a large number of pictures for a child to receive a real corn chip. The child is also eventually required to select a picture out of a large book, which can be unwieldy to carry and time-consuming to use and maintain. I remember that when Lucas used PECS I was constantly saying, "I need a new picture of pizza" or hearing the staff say, "We can't find Lucas's puzzle picture...we'll make a new one when we get a chance."

In addition, the PECS book has to accompany the child everywhere he goes, and it can be nearly useless for practicing mand trials while a child is in a pool or bouncing on a trampoline.

While I recommend sign language, I do want to say that if your child uses an augmentative system or voice output device successfully, don't discontinue its use abruptly. The key here is to evaluate how well your current system is working. You can do this by answering the following questions: Is the child able to use the system independently to request his needs and wants throughout the day (not just at snack time or when the device or book is placed within reach of the child)?; Is the child having tantrums or other problem behaviors because the system is overly cumbersome, breaks, or he is unable to use it fluently?; Does the child have access to the system across all environments and do both home and school providers use it consistently?

If you find by answering these questions that your child uses his device some times but not others, you might consider adding sign language to the mix for certain activities. For instance, if your child uses his voice output device or PECS at snack time, but doesn't take it to the pool or the trampoline, you might substitute sign language for those activities.

An eight-year-old I worked with a few years ago used a voice output device at times, was completely fluent with PECS, and used this as a back-up when his voice output system was broken (which seemed to be a lot of the time, to me!), and then we taught him to sign, too. Don't feel that you need to limit your child to just one device, as the goal is communication, not learning a system.

Becoming Proficient at Teaching Sign Language

Almost without exception, I recommend teaching children who are not yet vocal to use sign language either to supplement their current augmentative system or, if they currently have no system in place, to adopt sign language as the system they will learn and use functionally.

Your first step is to begin to teach yourself some signs immediately. Don't panic! You don't need to sign up for American Sign Language classes. You simply need to learn the signs for your child's top five to ten reinforcers and then you just need to learn a few additional signs to stay ahead of your child, including the signs for your child's reinforcers.

Once you've learned those signs you can begin to teach your child the signs. Once your child is fluent with two of the five mands, you can learn another two or three signs for preferred items (that will become the next mands) and begin teaching your child those signs. Honestly, learning the signs isn't hard. Teaching your child how to shape the signs is much more difficult. Here, I can only suggest that practice makes perfect—or at least will improve your skills! Actually, when it comes to teaching sign language, I don't necessarily think there is such a thing as doing it perfectly. It is really an artful dance, using the science of ABA, to shape better and better approximations.

To learn this complex dance, I have found that adult-to-adult role playing is the best way to learn how to teach children just about any skill, but it really works for sign language. One of the adults pretends to be the child and then a third adult can observe and offer comments. You'll need to learn how, when, how much, and what to accept as a correct response. Unfortunately, there is no concrete formula for teaching, since, just as in dancing, you will need to change and respond from moment to moment.

You'll find a balance between holding out for a perfect response and accepting errors, when you start working with your child. If your child becomes frustrated, you've pushed too far. However, if a child has never spoken and suddenly says "ca" as he reaches for a cookie, you'll want to reinforce this immediately.

If you're using sign language, everyone who works with the child needs to learn to sign the same words the same way, and you'll need to have frequent meetings and perhaps videotape some sessions to make sure that everyone is accepting the same signs. This will keep the child from becoming confused.

Teaching the First Five Signs

First and foremost, you need to invest in a good sign language dictionary. I like the book *Signing Exact English* (Gustason and Zawolkow 1993) and you'll find photos of 20 frequently used signs in Appendix 3 of this book. Another option is to surf the internet for sample sign language pictures and/or illustrations. One website that I would recommend is www.lifeprint.com.

Other valuable resources are the K and K Sign and Say Verbal Language Kit, developed by speech pathologists Nancy Kaufman and Tamara Kasper. These colorful flashcards depict pictures of the 150 most common reinforcers that children with autism and related disorders seem to enjoy. On the back of each card is an illustration and description of how to form the sign. Also on the back of each card is a breakdown of the word that helps guide non-speech therapists on how to have a child echo, starting at an immature level and growing incrementally to shape the word.

An example of the breakdown is for DVD (a highly preferred reinforcer for nearly all children with autism!). Before the child might be able to articulate DVD, according to Kaufman and Kasper, he should be able to say de-de, then de-be, then de-de-de, then de-be-de, then finally DVD. You can see an illustration of these cards and/or purchase them through www.northernspeechservices.com.

The next step in the process of teaching signs is to select the child's first five mands that you will teach, as well as the signs for your child's reinforcer. Some signs, such as "apple" and "candy" are considered signs that "rhyme" because the hand motions are similar (see the sample signs in Appendix 3). Start with five signs that are dissimilar, to make it easier for you and your child to shape the signs. If your child does have both "apple" and "candy" on his list of reinforcers, you'll probably want to look at a more specific sign for one of them, such as "lollipop" instead of "candy."

In addition you'll need to make sure that the signs are not too difficult to prompt and that the child will be able to eventually sign them without prompting. Some signs involve very complex fine motor skills that require dexterity that even typical children and adults would have trouble with. For these signs, feel free to simplify. For example, the sign for movie is fairly complex, but you can simplify it by having the child simply rub his hands together as if he was smashing Play Doh between them. Just make sure that all adults working with the child use the same simplified signs.

Now you're ready to start teaching. Begin by pairing the spoken word with the sign and the item. As you bring a chip closer to a child you'll say and sign "chip" three times before and during delivery. At this point, you are not prompting the child to move his hands or requiring him to say or sign anything. At this point you're pairing the word with the sign and the item, just as you would with vocal manding. Work on all five words together, not just one word at a time. Pairing might take just a few minutes or up to weeks, depending on how your child learns. And here's a reminder that your child should never know that he is working and you need to keep the motivation high and the demands very low as you work towards getting independent signing. So go slow and ease into any demands.

Next, you'll physically guide or prompt the child to produce the sign. If the cookie is a reinforcer and the child reaches for a cookie, Mom will show the child the sign for cookie as a demonstration as she is saying "cookie." Then Mom will gently take the child's hands and move them to sign "cookie" as she says cookie once again (prompt), and then Mom gives the child the piece of cookie, as she says "cookie" one last time. This same process is repeated for all the mands.

There are some positive things to look for during this process. I have seen many children very quickly start to independently use the signs when they see a preferred item. In addition, many of the children will start looking to the adult for a model and copying the sign without a physical prompt to get their reinforcement quicker. Finally, some children—even at this early stage—will begin to make word approximations while they are signing.

If your child does not begin to imitate or waits for you to prompt the correct signs by holding out their arms and displaying "zombie hands" (a phrase coined by Mr. Michael Miklos, Senior Behavior Analyst for the PA Verbal Behavior Project) you'll need to take action. Begin fading your prompts and accepting some approximations, just to get your child to be more independent.

I remember several years ago when Mike Miklos was helping me tackle a tough case with a young girl who was not becoming independent with her signing. This little girl was signing for popcorn, which is indicated by pointing both index fingers to the ceiling and moving both arms up and down. Mike pointed out that the little girl enjoyed when I pulled on her fingers and made the motion. She was not eager to sign "popcorn" because she was being reinforced not only by the popcorn but also by my prompt. Mike instructed me to accept her arms moving up and down as a mand and deliver the popcorn as soon as I saw her arms move even minimally. Within days we were able to shape the sign to truly look like the sign for popcorn. But even better, she was no longer prompt dependent for producing the sign and months later began to speak.

The opposite problem to "zombie hands" is when a child scrolls through all his signs like a baseball coach signaling the batter. While zombie hands is the result of over-prompting, scrolling (which we tend to see more often) is the result of fading prompts too quickly and reinforcing sloppy responses.

Never reinforce a child who scrolls. If you see a few signs scrolled together, even if the target sign is displayed in the bunch, you'll want to put the child's hands in a neutral position for one or two seconds so that you don't chain another sign with the error. Then you'll demonstrate the correct sign and prompt as much as needed to get the child to make the correct sign. Then you can reinforce.

After your child has several strong, independent signed mands, you can also begin to experiment with delaying reinforcement for a few seconds, holding out to see if you'll get some spoken word approximation. Don't hold out for more than a few seconds, though, as you have no control over your child's desire to speak.

Additional Ways to get Children to Talk

Teaching sign language in the context of a mand is the best way I know of to help a non-vocal or minimally vocal child, but there are other things that you can do to facilitate the talking as well.

First, you'll need to enrich your child's environment by bombarding your child with single words. When I go into home or school programs for the first time, I hear a lot of language, but most of it is too complex for non-vocal children to understand. Adults speak quickly and the child will often find this distorted and confusing. Imagine, again, that you are in a foreign country and someone is speaking to you quickly, using long sentences. You don't know the language, so it's impossible for you to catch the gist of the conversation.

Instead of saying, "John is going up the steps" as you and Johnny are walking upstairs, say, "Up, up, up" in a loud and playful voice. Try saying, "Tickle, tickle, tickle" instead of, "I'm going to tickle Johnny's belly." Whenever possible, pick single-syllable and easy words that might also serve as reinforcers. You don't have to learn the signs for all these words, just pair them three times with what's going on in your child's environment. One goal would be to pair the happy, playful tone of your voice with the word, which would then become a reinforcer.

Another way to make speech more reinforcing is to deliver reinforcers for any type of babbling, sounds, or word approximations that your child makes. To become aware of what sounds your child makes and how frequently he makes them, set a time for a specific period of time (15 minutes is good) and get a sheet of paper and write down what you hear. You will do this a few times to get a baseline. If you hear "ba da da" and then "oh" and then "ma ma" in a 15-minute period, you'll see that, while your child's babbling rate is low, his ability to put consonants and vowels together is quite good. Plus, the sounds he is making could be shaped into words. "Ba" could be a sheep sound, "mama" for Mom, "da da" for Dad, and "moo" for cow. This might also lead you to select reinforcers that use these same sounds. You can then make a conscious effort to reinforce your child for making these sounds. "Ba da ba Ryan, nice talking! You said ba da ba. Here, have a chip, you said ba da ba."

You can also try to encourage big movement activities before, during, and after the mand sessions. For some children, vigorous play and sensory activities often result in increased speech production. This is another opportunity to note what your child is doing when he begins to babble, to see if your child does babble more during gross motor activities.

Physically, you can also work to improve your child's mouth muscles. I've met parents who swear that their children became vocal at the age of five simply because of the use of a bubble, horn, and straw program developed by Talk Tools (www.talktools.net). Although there is no controlled research on its efficacy, it makes sense that strengthening the mouth muscles will aid in speech in the same way that strengthening arm muscles helps gross motor skills. These therapy tools also help the child to associate a controlled oral airflow with speech production. Sara Rosenfeld-Johnson, MS, CC-SLP, who created these oral motor tools and interventions, suggests that using progressively thinner straws and more difficult horns within a prescribed regimen does, in fact, result in more speech and better articulation.

Joanne Gerenser, a nationally known speech pathologist, observed Lucas once briefly when he was four years old and told me to throw away all of his sippy cups. She had seen Lucas running around his therapy room holding a sippy cup, and she let me know that the sippies deter articulation. They were, she told me, as bad as bottles and told me to encourage straw use, water bottle use, or open-cup drinking. All of this was to improve the muscle strength and control of the mouth.

Steps to Improve Articulation

If your child is beginning to put sounds together, using word approximations and maybe even has a few words, it's time to begin working on the clarity of the words so that strangers will understand him.

During my work with Lucas there were times when his articulation became sloppy. I remember that Gerenser commented about Lucas's pronunciation of the word "water." At that point in time, Lucas had begun to use the word "wah-yer" instead of "water." If pushed, he would articulate the word correctly, but most people who came in contact with Lucas, gave him water when he said "wah-yer." If the child can produce a word clearly, all adults must only accept and reinforce accurate vocalizations. The bar must be kept high and be inched up. This way, the child will become more, not less, understandable, over time.

Lucas also developed some articulation problems as he got a little older. For instance, he started saying "Mah-ye" instead of "Mommy." I discussed his sudden articulation decline with his ABA therapist who told me that the speech therapist at school would work on articulation, because it was not her area of expertise. So, it appeared again, that adults were accepting sloppy responses. To make matters worse my solution was to emphasize words and since Lucas is a very good imitator, he began to copy every word he heard. So I would say "Mooommm" and he would hear "Mama" because I overemphasized the last consonant and created an "a" sound on the end of almost every word. So, Lucas began to add an "a" to the end of each word he said: cup-a, spoon-a, etc. I felt like I had a little Italian boy in my house! Gerenser's advice was to start under-emphasizing the last consonant of the words and the problem cleared up almost instantly.

For children less vocal than Lucas, it's very important to keep a running list of what they are saying for each word, so you can help them to shape the word accurately. I like to go through flashcards and select single-syllable and double-syllable words that are fairly easy to say, such as cat, dog, bed, pop, puppy, mommy, apple, candy, etc. If I can find a handful or two of words that are fairly clear, I want to practice those words with the child throughout the day.

Separate the words into three piles: Clearly articulated words, words that need some work but have potential, and very difficult words. You'll start with the first pile and have the child practice those clearly articulated words several times per day with high amounts of reinforcement. You might then work in conjunction with a speech therapist to help you shape up the words in the second pile. Put the third pile away for now since you always want the child to be practicing words that are clear. If the child is practicing very difficult to pronounce words as tacts (labels), he is in essence practicing errors, which is not a good idea.

Getting a child to talk should be a team effort. It's everyone's job to help your child to speak, and to articulate well. Using these techniques consistently will improve nearly every child's chances of speaking and being understood. And, no matter how old the child or adult is, don't give up hope that someday he might become vocal. In the meantime, continue to help expand the child's language using a Verbal Behavior approach with the use of sign language.

CHAPTER 7

Errorless Teaching and the Use of Transfer Procedures

You've learned a lot about helping your child to communicate and have, I hope, begun to see some success in using reinforcers and in teaching mands. Now it's time to check your own progress in this program by making sure that you're working as effectively as possible with your child.

In this chapter we're going to take a closer look at prompting, prompt fading, transferring skills across operants, and error correction. Success with a Verbal Behavior (VB) program often depends on the crisp understanding and deliverance of these concepts.

Prompting

Prompts are the little nudges or hints that will increase the likelihood of a correct response from your child. The difference between a great Applied Behavior Analysis (ABA)/VB program and a mediocre program is often in the details of correct prompting procedures.

I've mentioned prompting throughout the book thus far, so it's a term with which you're probably familiar. But there are different types of prompts, prompt fading, and correction procedures that need further explanation.

It's important when teaching a child with autism or any developmental delay that you not only know the science of ABA and the conceptual analysis of VB, but also that you can deliver accurate and appropriate therapy.

When Lucas was three, we began our first ABA/Lovaas program and our behavior consultant spent two days with us before limiting her visits to once a month. Since she had been highly trained by professionals working directly under Dr. Lovaas, she provided a wealth of guidance on prompting and prompt fading. Each of Lucas's therapists and I would get in the chair and work directly with Lucas in front of her and the other team members. She critiqued us if we prompted too quickly or too much, or if we reinforced too late. She recommended that I serve as Lucas's therapist for at least three hours a week, so that I could practice and become proficient as a behavioral technician (this was before I began any education to become a Board Certified Behavior Analyst or BCBA). Her feedback helped me to excel in this area.

Prompt Hierarchy

The basics of prompting include the several different types of prompts, and a hierarchy to identify how invasive the prompt is. You'll want to use the least intrusive prompt that will still allow your child to be successful.

The most invasive type of prompt for a physical response is a full physical prompt, which means that you take the child's hand or body and move it so that he correctly responds to whatever direction is given. So, if the child is told to touch his nose, but appears to have no idea what that means and has no ability to imitate, the instructor will take the child's hand and prompt his finger to touch his nose. This is a "full physical prompt."

A "partial physical prompt" is similar, but the instructor's help is limited to touching the child's elbow or moving his hands towards his face, and the child finishes the request by touching his own nose, by himself.

Gestural prompts include pointing to an item and are less invasive, simply because they don't involve touching the child. Gestural prompts can be used both in intensive training sessions, as well as during normal daily activities, such as when Katie doesn't follow an instruction to put on her coat. If Katie doesn't respond to your instruction, you prompt her by repeating your request and pointing towards her coat. If Katie has poor listening abilities and putting on her coat is a new skill, you will probably have to start by using a physical prompt, and fade to a less invasive gestural prompt as quickly as you can.

A "model or imitative prompt" is even less intrusive. If the child is told to touch his nose, the teacher may try and touch her own nose to give the child an idea of what they are looking for. If the child imitates the move, this is the preferable prompt. This prompt can also fade to a "partial imitative prompt." The teacher may only have to start moving her finger towards her own nose before the child gets the idea and complies.

Other prompts that are used in VB programs include visual and textual prompts. These are technically considered less invasive than modeling/imitative types of prompts but, for some skills, such as receptive and matching skills, modeling may be the lowest-level prompt you will use. The primary advantage to using visual and textual prompts is that an adult does not have to always be present to deliver the prompt. A visual schedule is an example of a visual prompt which the child can be taught to manage. These schedules can often lead to increased independent skills for down time and self-care activities.

Visual prompts can also be used with an adult present. If your child uses sign language to facilitate communication, the teacher should initially sign the words while giving the direction. This would be a visual prompt. If you tell a signing child to "get ball" you should sign "ball" while you are giving the instruction.

A textual prompt is useful for more advanced learners or typical learners and would include showing the child the word "ball" while giving the verbal direction, "Get ball."

Verbal prompts are considered to be the least invasive type of prompt and are used frequently throughout the day—sometimes, too much, in my opinion. They oftentimes become ineffective with children who have severe language delays. One form of verbal prompting is to repeat the direction and give reminders; a strategy that often resembles nagging. If the student doesn't have the language or the cognitive abilities to understand the direction, no amount of nagging is going to get the desired result. Unfortunately, some teachers believe that by speaking more loudly and using more description in their request that the student will understand. For example, Jimmy may be told to, "Go get your shoes." When he doesn't comply, the incorrect verbal prompt becomes, "Jimmy, I told you to go get your shoes and bring them upstairs…we have to go!" As you know by now, less is more and the fewer words used, the easier it is for the child to process.

Adults also use verbal prompts by emphasizing one word of a sentence, such as "touch NOSE." Most children who do not understand the direction "touch nose" aren't going to suddenly understand it if "nose" is said louder. These children will often need a more invasive prompt in order to learn the skill. Remember, you want to select the prompt that will work best the first time. You don't want to yell "touch NOSE" and get a bunch of non-responses before moving into a physical or imitative prompt. It is far better to start with a more invasive prompt, and fade the prompt out quickly.

I learned early on to keep the demands simple and clear. You want only one antecedent. If you give your child the command, "Touch your nose," that's your antecedent, while you wait for the behavior and then you provide the consequence. You'll want to use the least intrusive prompt within the antecedent condition to get the child to comply, and you don't want to add additional tasks or language to the request. I commonly see adults re-presenting the demand over and over, with no prompting.

Shortly after Lucas began ABA therapy, my husband started to ask him to get the remote control. At that time, Lucas had no idea what a remote control was and was unable to complete the task, nor could he follow the direction by following my husband's point. My husband continued to offer the same verbal prompt over and over again, while offering the same partial gestural prompt over and over again.

There were too many antecedents, and the prompting was not invasive enough, so Lucas could not complete the task and ran off to do something he wanted to do. Unfortunately the task wasn't completed and because he ran off to do what he liked, his non-compliance was actually reinforced.

When giving an instruction it's best to give only one antecedent, expect only one behavior, and deliver only one consequence. Giving too much information, or escalating the amount of information given, will reinforce your child's sloppy responses and possibly teach him that it's all right to tune you out or disobey you, to get a reaction.

Begin making demands on your child that are super simple, can be completed with the most minimally intrusive prompting, and can be rewarded immediately. Giving the direction to toss a ball through a basketball hoop may not seem at all like work to your child, but when you reward the compliance, he's learning that following directions will get him something that he wants. Prompting should also seem natural and be as gentle as possible. If your child doesn't throw the ball through the hoop, approach him and re-state the request, and then playfully take his arms and help him toss the ball, and then deliver reinforcement.

This way, your child learns that compliance brings him rewards.

Once your child is responding to the prompts on a regular basis, you'll need to fade the prompts out in order for your child to progress. If you don't, your child will become prompt dependent and will not become an independent learner.

Errorless Teaching and Transfer Trials Within Operants

Teaching your child new skills is an exciting time, especially when you see the fruits of your hard work. I've learned in recent years that it's really important to use zero-second prompting when you're working on a new skill, or with a new child. What this means is that if you think that there is even a small chance that the child is going to give the wrong answer or not perform the requested task, you'll need to prompt immediately. Once it appears to you that the child is beginning to understand the task, you can begin to fade the prompt. You'll fade these prompts by doing a transfer trial immediately after prompted trials.

I had an "a-ha" moment about four years ago when I learned about transfer trials. Lucas was already six years old and had been in a home ABA program for three years when I heard about transfer trials at a VB hands-on training workshop presented by Holly Kibbe and Cherish Twiggs. Prior to that workshop, I sometimes thought that Lucas had aphasia, a condition common to stroke victims, where they cannot find the correct word for a situation. I had seen it during my nursing years and it seemed to me that Lucas had a similar issue. If Lucas wanted a pretzel from the cabinet he'd gesture for me to open the door. Even though the pretzels, cookies, and crackers were in plain view once the cabinet door was opened, Lucas wouldn't say "pretzel" to ask for what he wanted. So, I would say "pretzel," and Lucas would echo "pretzel" and I'd deliver the pretzel and that would be that.

Once I learned about transfer procedures, though, it became clear that Lucas did not have aphasia. *I* was the problem! I was leaving all of his responses at the prompt level and not completing a transfer trial. Once I got home from the workshop, I was eager to try my new plan. Instead of handing over a pretzel to Lucas immediately after he echoed my verbal prompt, I would hesitate and shrug my shoulders, or else (if I had to) say, "What do you want?" He would need to say "pretzel" again, before getting the pretzel.

Getting Lucas to say "pretzel" independently or with a reduced prompt became the new goal. I worked hard on this concept and published a controlled research study I conducted with Lucas in the journal *The Analysis of Verbal Behavior*, in 2005.

I now think about this skill in two ways: Transfer trials *within* operants and transfer trials *across* operants. A transfer trial within an operant is the transfer of stimulus control from a prompted trial to a trial with a diminished prompt, to no prompt at all. That would include the above prompt-fading scenario with Lucas and the pretzels.

Here are two more examples of transfer trials within one skill area or one operant. I want Susie to learn a receptive skill, such as responding appropriately to the direction: "Clap your hands." At this point, though, Susie has no receptive skills at all, and cannot comply with the request. I would begin immediately with a full physical prompt, where I take Susie's hands and physically bring them together in a clap. If I immediately reinforce the skill with an M&M (a very strong reinforcer), I'd be leaving the skill at a very high prompt level and would not be providing any sort of transfer trial. Instead, I recommend that the prompt be faded or eliminated before reinforcement is provided. So, instead of giving Susie an M&M after I helped her clap her own hands, I would give her praise (a lesser reinforcer) and then re-present the command: "Great...clap your hands" and see if she'll do it. I'd continue offering praise until Susie responds to a lesser prompt and then I'd give her the stronger reinforcer of the M&M.

Here's how it would look:

> Instructor: "Clap your hands." Immediately takes Susie's hands and claps them together.
>
> Susie: Claps her hands with a full physical prompt from the instructor.
>
> Instructor: "Right...clap your hands..." Touches Susie's elbows and forearms.

Susie: Claps her hands.

Instructor: Delivers M&M while smiling and saying "Good clapping hands."

Here's an example of a transfer trial for a tact (label). Sam is an intermediate vocal learner who has hundreds of known tacts but cannot tact "bulldozer." Here is a transfer trial for that:

Instructor: "What is it? Bulldozer."

Sam: "Bulldozer."

Instructor: "Right...what is it?"

Sam: "Bulldozer."

Instructor: Delivers praise and a short clip of a favorite DVD.

In addition to transferring stimulus control from a heavily prompted trial to less of a prompt, you can also work on using transfer trials to be used across operants.

I got interested in researching transfer procedures across operants in 2001. When Lucas was six or seven years old, he went to an ABA school that was about an hour away from my house. After Lucas had been at the school about four months, I noticed that he was using the teachers' names improperly. When his therapist Amber came to our house, she would say "Bye, Lucas" as she was leaving. Lucas would respond, "Bye Haley" (Haley was his teacher at school). Amber would correct him, saying, "No, I'm not Haley, say Bye Amber." Then Lucas would say, "Bye Amber." She would leave, without completing a trial transfer (unfortunately). At that time I was completing course work for my behavior analyst certificate and quickly realized what was going on, and that we needed to do something about it. We had worked quite diligently on his greeting skills in the past, and tacting people's names was actually a strength for Lucas. I remember when he went to his typical preschool, we taught him the names of all 16 of his classmates. What appeared to be happening at the ABA school was that Lucas never learned the names of staff and students and, by adding greetings to work on generalization, Lucas was making errors. That, in turn, caused much confusion. It was clearly a programming error, and so we took immediate steps to correct it. Whenever I look at errors like this, I will look to see if the prerequisite skills are met. Is the base solid? How can we break down this skill so that Lucas would be successful?

In this case, I looked back to when he was successful learning and using his classmates' names. I remembered that we had taught him to tact the kids names by showing him pictures of the children—one child in each picture—in a drill-like fashion.

I asked his teacher at the ABA school to send home pictures of ten staff members and/or students in Lucas's class. This was at the beginning of a two-week break, and I told the teacher that my goal for Lucas would be that he would learn all ten names by the time he returned to school. So each day I took the pack of pictures and would go through them one at a time, asking "Who's this?"

Based on this "cold probe" (an assessment prior to any teaching) I picked three targets that I would work on. I would lay those three pictures on the table and would tell Lucas, "Touch Amber." He would then touch the picture of Amber, and would also usually echo "Amber" as he touched the photo. I would then immediately transfer this listener skill to a tact by saying, "Right...who is this?" and then Lucas would respond "Amber."

I spent five or ten minutes each day teaching Lucas the names. Prior to each teaching session I'd cold probe all ten pictures to see if he was acquiring any tacting skills, and then I would select three new targets for the session as soon as he was naming the target tacts on the cold probe. In just two weeks Lucas learned all ten names and could use them fluently with no hesitation. And not only did Lucas return after two weeks knowing all the names of his classmates and staff, he was also able to attach a greeting to the names too.

This proved to me that this is the way that Lucas learns best, and it led me to set up a few structured research studies with Lucas and other children to look at the issue of transferring stimulus across operants. I wanted to focus on what had happened during those two weeks that was so successful for Lucas. I discovered that I was taking Lucas's receptive language skills, which had always been stronger than his expressive skills, and transferring the stimulus control (the names of his classmates) from the receptive operant to the tacting operant. When I examined the process I had used, I discovered that I was also mixing in an echoic to tact transfer.

Completing transfer trials across operants is something I use on a daily basis with all children I work with, whether or not they are vocal (sign language is extremely useful in this task, for non-vocal children).

Here are some examples of transfer trials across operants:

Receptive to Tact Transfer

Instructor: "Touch bulldozer."

Student: Touches picture of bulldozer (receptive).

Instructor: "What is it?"

Student: "Bulldozer" (tact).

Echoic to Tact Transfer

Instructor: "Say ball."

Student: "Ball" (echoic).

Instructor: Holds up a picture of a ball and says, "What is it?"

Student: "Ball" (tact).

Match to Sample to Receptive Transfer

Instructor: "Match cat" while handing a picture of a cat to student.

Student: Matches cat (match to sample).

Instructor: "Touch cat."

Student: Touches cat (receptive).

Tact to Intraverbal Transfer

Instructor: "What number?" holding up the number 9 on a flash-card.

Student: "Nine" (tact).

Instructor: "How old are you?" Fade out the visual, if possible.

Student: "Nine" (intraverbal).

The transfer trial procedure across operants is a useful way to build on the child's strengths and help improve his weak areas.

Error Correction

Even children who have some good skills will make mistakes, so it's important to be ready to prompt immediately; even then, your child will make mistakes. The way you treat errors can either help or hinder your child's progress. It's a little scary, but you must teach everyone in your child's environment how to properly correct errors.

Unfortunately, this is unrealistic, so you can just assume that some of your child's errors will unwittingly be reinforced. I often see intermediate learners who call a picture of a pool "swimming," or when asked to name a chalkboard, reply "teacher." It's not that these learners don't know the answer or have some cognitive problems that are preventing them from learning the correct tacts, it's that these errors have been reinforced many times in the past.

This is how you correct errors:

Let's take the example of an eight-year-old child named Andrew. He has autism, is vocal, and can mand and tact pictures of several reinforcers. You are now beginning to teach him to tact pictures of common items. The target tact is a bed. This tact frequently needs to be taught, because when Andrew sees a picture of a bed and is asked, "What is it?" he replies "Blanket."

If a child responds with a wrong answer, it's actually more difficult to teach the tact than if the child doesn't respond at all. Although close, words like "blanket" for "bed" or "sit" instead of "chair" are reinforced by parents and others in the environment who will try to manipulate a correct answer from an incorrect answer. If shown a picture of a chair, and the child says "Sit," the instructor who is not familiar with proper error correction procedures might respond, "Well, you do sit in a chair, right. It's a chair." But since the child never said "Chair," the word "Sit" is reinforced.

To correct errors such as this you'll need to hold up the picture of the bed again, or point to a real bed and state the direction again: "What is it?" You must immediately prompt with the word "Bed," before Andrew has the opportunity to say "Blanket." Andrew will echo the word "bed," and then you can perform a transfer trial to get him from the echoic operant to the tact, by saying, "Right—what is it?" When asked the question this time, you can either reduce the prompt (for instance you could begin to say the word b___ although you do need to be careful with the partial verbal prompt since both blanket and bed begin with the b sound) or by waiting to see if Andrew produces the word with no prompting at all.

Here's how error correction for Andrew will look:

Instructor: Holds up a picture of a bed and says, "What is it?"

Andrew: "Blanket."

Instructor: Holds up the picture of the bed again and re-presents the question and immediately prompts the answer, "Bed."

Andrew: Echoes "Bed," based on the verbal prompt of the instructor.

Instructor: "Right—what is it?"

Andrew: "Bed," with no prompt.

Errors occur within the natural environment, too. A common problem that young children with autism or other language impairment exhibit, is that they tend to reverse pronouns. So if you say, "Roll the ball to me," they might echo, "Roll the ball to me" as they are rolling it to you. Or if you say "Brush your hair," your child will echo back, "Brush your hair," as he is following the direction. The simple solution to this problem is to eliminate pronouns, especially if your child echoes a lot. Simply say, "Roll ball" or "Brush hair." When your child is more advanced, you can prompt the appropriate pronoun. When working with your child always take your child's perspective so when he says, "Give you a cookie," prompt, "Give me a cookie" and have him echo that response and then do a transfer trial by saying, "Right! Now you ask me." Once he successfully says, "Give me a cookie" without an immediate prompt, deliver the cookie as reinforcement.

Do not deliver reinforcement with the pronoun reversal or you will see those errors increase, as do all behaviors that are reinforced.

Learning the best way to prompt, fade prompts, correct errors, and transfer skills across operants are essential tools in your arsenal to teach your child and can be practiced anywhere. It may sound a bit overwhelming, but remember that you, too, are susceptible to reinforcement and you'll feel better once your child begins to respond to you more accurately.

CHAPTER 8

Teaching Receptive Language Skills and Other Nonverbal Operants

When Lucas began his Lovaas Applied Behavior Analysis (ABA) program in 1999, the first skills we worked on were receptive, imitation, and matching skills. Even though Lucas had about 100 words in his vocabulary, including several mands and intraverbal fill-ins, we started where the Lovaas protocol mandated, and that was with these nonverbal skills. Skinner describes receptive language as listener skills and doesn't focus at all on developing imitation and matching skills, since he doesn't consider them "verbal behavior."

But that doesn't mean they aren't important. In current Verbal Behavior (VB) programs, teaching children to respond to these nonverbal operants is important and occurs early in the programming. These programs are great to start with because they are easy to prompt (because there is no talking involved on the part of the child) and all children need to learn how to follow directions (receptive skills), to participate in a VB program. The first directions that you give a child should always be simple enough for him to follow—or that you can assess he's not following. The beauty of the receptive skills is that they don't require a child to speak and many children find them easy to comply with. The bonus is that you can build momentum in all your programs because even a minor response from your child will be rewarded.

Teaching these skills can often turn the tide away from non-compliance and frustration to learning!

Teaching Receptive or Listener Skills

I recently heard Dr. Mark Sundberg speak, and he has replaced the term "receptive skills" with the term "listener skills." Dr. Sundberg said that Julie Vargas, B.F. Skinner's daughter, had been trying for years to get him to change the terminology because Skinner believed that the term "receptive" was too cognitive. In the same way that he thought the word "expressive" was too vague to describe manding, tacting, intraverbals, and echoics, he believed that "developing listener skills" was a better way to describe the process of assessing and developing this skill.

Receptive language or listener skills include being able to respond to another person's direction. A child with receptive skills will respond appropriately when you say, "Clap your hands," or, "Get in line," or, "Put on your shoes." Even before a typical child can speak, he will be able to follow instructions to get a tissue, find the remote control, or point to Mommy. If you look at milestones for typically developing kids (www.firstsigns.org has a list) you'll see that receptive language is strong even before a child is a year old.

Children with autism usually don't have strong listener skills when they are diagnosed, since these skills are either very delayed or in some cases regress after one year of age. You've probably noticed that your child might not always respond when his name is called, or when you ask him to get his shoes. He also might not be able to follow simple commands such as, "Clap your hands" or, "Touch your head."

Lucas had very little receptive language prior to starting ABA. I noticed this particularly when my son Spencer was born when Lucas was 18 months old. I remember telling friends that Lucas just didn't "get it" and was oblivious to the new baby. When I had a photographer come to our house to take pictures shortly after Spencer came home from the hospital, the photographer handed Lucas a film canister and asked him to throw it in the trash. Lucas threw the canister on the floor and ran around in circles.

A few months later, soon after Lucas's second birthday, when it was clear he needed speech therapy, I wrote on his assessment form that he could touch his body parts upon request. Later I realized that he did this only when I read him a Barney book about body parts, while he followed along touching his head, nose, knees, and toes in the same order. In the absence of the Barney book, Lucas's ability to receptively identify his body parts was poor.

The good news for those of you starting a program is that once we did begin our ABA program with Lucas his receptive language skills grew quickly. For Lucas, an ability to follow directions and other receptive language skills are now strengths.

Improving Receptive Language Skills within the Natural Environment

Prompting, which was discussed in Chapter 7, is an important intervention to follow when you're teaching your child to follow through with directions.

As I mentioned in previous chapters, do not link your child's name to demands. Responding to their own name is a skill that many children with autism do not possess. Limiting the use of your child's name will actually help him to learn to respond when his name is called, because he won't tune it out as part of a long list of demands.

Here's my strategy for getting your child to respond to his name:

Dennis hardly ever responds to his name. First, tell everyone in the environment to stop using, or limit the use of his name throughout the day. Then get several of Dennis's strongest consumable or controllable reinforcers (chips and bubbles, for instance) and go behind him when he's engaged in another activity. Call his name while standing just a few feet behind him and then immediately touch his shoulder, turn him around, and hand him a chip. Gradually fade your prompt by standing a little further away and delay touching his shoulder by a second or two. Dennis will learn that when he hears his name, good things happen. Working on responding to his name in this way can be done throughout the day, whenever you are able to deliver reinforcement.

In fact when you're working on listening skills, only give directions if you're willing to follow through with prompting. Don't bombard your child with constant demands, either. This program is intended to be easy in the beginning to build confidence for you and your child. Toward that end, also make sure that you are giving lots of positive talk for every negative comment or correction, as suggested by Dr. Glen Latham. He prescribes eight positive comments for every negative comment. Everyone needs to be on board with this program: your spouse, your baby-sitter, and your mother-in-law.

If everyone is working together you'll see your child begin to follow simple directions in a short period of time. If not, you'll continue to see spikes in problem behaviors and non-compliance. If that's the case, you can find out who is not following your protocol by observing your child interacting with adults and clicking off the number of positive comments on a counter, and the number of negatives on another. Share your data with that person, and then ask him or her to watch you interact with the child and collect another set of clicks. In general I have found that people easily overestimate how positive they are and underestimate the abundance of their negative comments.

Teaching Listener Skills with Intensive Teaching Sessions

When doing intensive teaching sessions I recommend that you have a fair number of targeted listener skills before you begin. I suggest starting several receptive programs during intensive teaching, such as following directions, receptive body parts, and receptive identification.

Each program will need at least two targets, so that you'll know if your child can differentiate between them. When I was just getting started with consulting, a mom brought her two-year-old son Daniel to my home. She was very proud of the fact that Daniel now clapped his hands at the request "Clap hands" and that skill was now in his maintenance book. It had taken Daniel months to respond to that target, so Mom was especially disappointed when I told her that to truly be mastered, Daniel would have to demonstrate that he could discriminate between two or more targets.

It comes down to this: When you teach a child with autism one skill in isolation, giving them tons of reinforcement for that one skill, you'll find it very difficult to teach them a second or third skill. When the therapist said "Clap hands," Daniel very likely heard "dah dah." So when "Stand up" became the target, he also heard "dah dah." When you put them together, Daniel had a 50/50 chance of getting it right to receive his reinforcement. He didn't really learn to hear "Clap hands," at all. If you pick at least two targets per program, the child receives prompting and reinforcement from the start for correct differentiation.

Clap hands, stomp feet, stand up, sit down, tap table, jump, turn around, raise arms, and fold hands are all good targets for your intensive teaching sessions. If your child can already comply with any of these simple commands, write each mastered target on an index card so you can begin to mix in targets he does know with targets he's just learning.

Once you have a list of the targets he knows, you can assess or probe how he's doing at the beginning of your teaching session, too (see the probe sheet in Appendix 5).

Let's say you're trying to teach your child to respond correctly to the requests "Clap hands," "Stomp feet," and "Stand up."

Before any teaching takes place, you'll pick one of these targets (not always the same one; mix up the order) and assess whether the child can correctly respond to the direction without any prompting. If you say "Stomp feet," make sure to keep your eyes from glancing at the child's feet, as that would be a prompt. During a cold probe, you need to be careful to do no prompting at all. Don't raise your voice or glance at the child's hands for "Clap hands," or touch the child in any way. Then record his response by circling the "Yes" or "No" on your probe sheet. A "Yes" would only be circled if the child responded appropriately with no prompting. Then assess the other two targets.

Here's an example of how to conduct a cold probe for a receptive skill:

> Instructor: "Clap hands," said in a neutral tone with no prompts.
>
> Child: Bangs her hand on the table.
>
> Instructor: Circles "No" on the probe sheet.

Now that the probe is done for those targets, you can begin teaching these targets. You'll be using both prompt fading and transfer procedures to accomplish these goals. When I consult in established home or school Verbal Behavior programs and see probe sheets with lots of "No's" on it, I ask how much teaching has been done after the probes. I find it useful to then watch the teaching sessions to see if there are problems with transferring or prompt fading.

As I discussed in Chapter 7, when you begin teaching a new skill, you may have to use a full physical prompt and then fade to a full imitative prompt and then a partial imitative prompt. You'll need to "hit" each target several times within the teaching session to have a good chance of getting a correct response on the following day's cold probe. Probing is an important assessment tool, but you've got to teach for a fair amount each day for each of your targets.

Here is how you will teach a receptive command such as "Stomp feet": Before giving a direction, such as "Stomp feet" or "Stand up," you must position the child so that you are face to face, both sitting in chairs. This is important because if your child is sitting at a table and then you give the direction "Stomp feet" and then pull the chair away from the table, you'll be prompting your child. Remember you're working on listening skills. You are not teaching your child to understand your physical cues, so do not give any visual prompts.

> Instructor: "Stomp feet." Immediately put hands gently on child's knees and make feet go up and down in a full physical prompt of the stomping action.
>
> Child: Stomps feet with a full physical prompt from the instructor.
>
> Instructor: "Right…stomp feet…" touches child's knees slightly.
>
> Child: Stomps feet with a reduced prompt.
>
> Instructor: Delivers M&M while smiling and saying, "Good stomping feet."
>
> Instructor: "Clap hands."

The next skill to work on—or even at the same time, since it's very similar to listening skills—is a receptive body parts program. If you combine programs, you can choose three targets, such as "Clap hands," "Stomp feet," and "Touch head." The body parts program will teach your child to touch different body parts on command. Start with big body parts and choose areas that are not too close to each other. Choosing belly and head would be good, while selecting nose and eyes would probably be too close to each other as beginning targets.

Cold probe the targets before you begin teaching, just as you did for the receptive commands. Also, as with listening skills, body part skills take a careful mixture of prompting, prompt fading, and transfer procedures.

Here's an example of how to teach receptive body parts to a child who can imitate:

> Instructor: "Touch head," and then immediately model by touching their own head.

Child: Touches head, following the model.

Instructor: "Good touching head," while removing their hand from their head and putting it in a neutral position.

Instructor: "Touch head," with no prompt.

Child: Touches head.

Instructor: "Touch belly," then immediately models touching their own belly.

Both of those examples show that it's important to switch between the targets during the teaching. Don't focus on "Touch head" ten times in a row and then move on to "Touch belly." You need to teach your child how to listen to your words and learn how to discriminate from the beginning.

The third receptive program I'm going to describe is receptive identification (receptive ID). If your child has no receptive ability, you will have to start with putting just one item on a table and asking the child to touch it. For instance, you might put a baby shoe on the table and say, "Touch shoe." Then, hold the shoe up in the air and tell the child to "Touch shoe" again. Your child may need to learn what "touch" means.

Once your child has that skill down pat (or if he is beginning the teaching with some receptive ability) teach him to discriminate between two items or two pictures and then slowly add to the number of items on the table. Many children do better with identifying the actual items, but I have seen a few who do better with pictures at first. Eventually you'll be using both pictures and items.

When you did your assessment (described in Chapter 3) I encouraged you to begin to gather a clear box of 3D items that could be used for matching as well as for receptive identification. You'll need these items handy for this phase of your teaching.

You'll also want to put together a container of reinforcing objects that your child can mand for, as well as two identical photos of each of these items. You can take pictures of the actual items, or you can go to www.google.com and, under the images tab, type in the item you're looking for. Click on the images tab to find and copy a picture that way. You can use these items and pictures to teach all of the operants.

Let's use Robert to show you how to begin this teaching. Robert can touch one reinforcing item when it is held in different positions, as well as when it's laying on the table. But Robert tends to want to touch and play with his reinforcing items, so for him it's best to start with putting two or three common (non-reinforcing) items on the table and assessing which of the items he can touch without a prompt.

You'll need to have at least three items to work with. Even if Robert can touch the shoe when you say "Touch shoe" and can also touch the cup when you say "Touch cup," it's not certain that Robert has mastered those targets. With only two things on the table, there's a 50/50 chance that he'll be correct. If you have three or preferably more items, you'll know better if your child has mastered the target.

As you're working with your child, you'll make the items more similar as he progresses, testing shoe versus sandal, or cup versus bottle. Once the item is mastered in a field of three items, then you will increase the number of items on the table until your child can identify the item in a field of six or more items.

The teaching procedure for receptive identification is a mixture of transfer procedures and carefully fading prompts.

Robert is learning receptive identification in a field size of three items, and we'll be using actual 3D items to work on his skills. When working on this with your child, be careful not to position the cards or items the same way, and mix the cards around within each teaching session. Pay attention to see which cards your child is choosing to assess if he's choosing only the center card or the left or right card. Make sure your placement of the cards isn't neat, either, because that may trigger the child to become obsessive during the session and start displaying problem behaviors.

> Instructor: Puts an actual shoe, cup, or car on the table, says "Touch car" and immediately points to or touches the car (gestural prompt).
>
> Robert: Touches car.
>
> Instructor: "Right, touch car."
>
> Robert: Touches car without a prompt.
>
> Instructor: "Where's your head?" (A known skill.)
>
> Robert: Touches head.
>
> Instructor: "Good, where's the car?" with no prompt.
>
> Robert: Touches car.

Instructor: Turns on DVD player for a short snippet of a movie, and gives Robert praise.

Tossing in known skills ("Where's your head," in the above example) is called a "distractor trial," and your child may be ready fairly early in your teaching sessions for distracter trials. This helps to separate the prompted trial for receptive identification from the independent trial. The goal here is that during tomorrow's probe, Robert will get the response correct without any prompts. Giving him practice responding more independently during the session, by throwing in known responses, may help him achieve that goal.

Teaching Imitation Skills

Typically developing children find it easy to imitate, and no effort is needed to teach them this skill. Children with autism, however, usually have a core deficit in their ability to imitate others, and usually have extremely poor imitation skills. You usually won't see them imitating other toddlers playing with toys, or imitating their parents doing chores, or imitating the other children's hand motions during circle time in preschool.

An ability to imitate is an extremely important skill to teach children who have a deficit in this area. In Lovaas ABA programs, gross motor imitation, which involves movements such as stomping feet or clapping hands, are taught first. Lovaas consultants then recommend moving on to fine motor imitation and then to oral motor imitation and then finally to vocal imitation. This was the sequence used to teach Lucas, who started with no imitation skills, nor any ability to echo on command. While the sequence did work, it was months before we got to verbal imitation drills.

I also take imitation very seriously when using the Verbal Behavior approach. However, you don't have to wait until motor imitation skills are solid to start working on echoic or verbal imitation skills. I'll address the echoic operant in the next chapter, but now it's time for you to learn how to teach motor imitation skills.

There are two imitation programs that I usually start for a beginning learner: toy/object imitation and gross motor imitation. A common criticism of both Verbal Behavior and Lovaas ABA programs is that they don't focus enough on play skills. In fact, critics complain that all we are interested in is drilling language and that young children learn everything—including language—through play. However, as a behavior analyst, I've come to believe that not all children like toys and may have no idea how to pretend play or have any interest in play at all. I know that I'm going to have to teach play skills just as I have taught language skills. I do this the same way I do all lessons—I pair toys that the child has low interest in, with high reinforcers.

Toy imitation is a great way to start. This can be started even with a beginning learner and is easily incorporated into your manding program. Toys are also great because children will see you being playful and will have no idea that they are doing work.

Start with baby toys, if that's where the interest is for your child. Get out your hammer and ball set, your spinning tops, and your pop-up toys. Other good toys to begin with are teacups and spoons, Fisher Price play figures, a farm or dollhouse, and toy cars. Begin the program by having two identical sets of your toys, so that you and your child will each have a set. Give the direction "Do this" while performing the activity, such as making the car go back or forth on the rug, or stirring the spoon in the teacup. Next, immediately take your child's hand and prompt the action with his set of the item. Then begin to fade the prompt, as you have with all your teaching thus far.

Pick just a few targets to start. You may want to say "Do this," and stir the spoon in your teacup, prompt, and fade, and then give the direction "Do this," and pretend to feed a doll with the spoon. This type of teaching helps your child learn to discriminate between the different uses for the spoon. If you select only one target with the spoon in the teacup, your child will most likely see the teacup and spoon, hear "Do this," and pick up the spoon and stir it.

Here's an example, with Kelly:

> Instructor: "Do this," while rolling the car back and forth, and then immediately providing full physical prompt to help Kelly roll her car back and forth.
>
> Kelly: Rolls her car back and forth with a prompt.
>
> Instructor: "Right, do this," while rolling car back and forth (points to Kelly's car or provides partial physical prompt, if needed).

Kelly: Rolls car back and forth with gestural prompt.

Instructor: "Great job…here's some crayons and paper." (Preferred items.)

In addition to a toy imitation program, I recommend that you start a motor imitation program. It's not a bad idea to select responses that you are also targeting for your receptive, command, and body parts program. These skills will transfer easily between operants and will facilitate mastering the targets. When doing this, please make sure that you're probing accurately. One of the first times I was in a Verbal Behavior classroom I watched one of the teachers assessing a child's abilities. She was saying "Clap hands" while she was clapping her own hands. I stopped her and asked which operant she was assessing. If she had been assessing the receptive skill, she should not have been providing a visual model of the action. If she was assessing the imitation skill, she should not be giving the auditory prompt of saying "Clap hands." Assessing each skill must be done separately.

Imitation skills are always assessed with the command, "Do this." Once the probe is completed, though, the real advantage to picking the same targets is revealed. During teaching you can use transfer procedures across the operants so you'll probably see your child able to master targets more quickly and generalize better.

Here's an example of teaching a motor imitation skill with Julie:

Instructor: "Do this," while clapping hands, and giving a partial physical prompt.

Julie: Claps her hands.

Instructor: "Right—do this," while clapping hands.

Julie: Claps hands with no prompt.

Instructor: "Do this," and touches head with both hands.

Julie: Touches her head with both hands (no prompt as this was a previously known skill).

Instructor: "Great!—Do this," and claps hands.

Julie: Claps hands with no prompt.

Instructor: "Awesome job," and tickles Julie with a big feather.

Teaching Visual Performance/Matching Skills

The last skill area that is not a verbal operant is the visual performance area. The beginner skills in this area include puzzle-building skills as well as matching identical objects and pictures.

It's time to gather your boxes of identical items as well as two sets of identical flashcards. Some children do best with these skills when you use items (real or pictures) that are strong reinforcers.

When assessing these matching skills you'll want to use the words "match" or "put with same" or use no words and hand them one card at a time.

When I teach this skill, however, I find it useful to always use the item name and use the sign if the child uses sign language instead of, or in addition to, the word "match." This helps imbed language and simple words into the child's programming. It's possible that your child will begin to pick up the item's name and will be more able to receptively identify it, if they hear the words frequently. Your child might even begin to echo your words as a result of pairing the word so frequently with the matching activity.

Here's how teaching this skill would look, working with Josh and three items on the table:

> Instructor: Places spoon, plastic Barney figurine and a small, soft cat on a table. Then hands Josh another identical Barney figurine and says "Barney" while gesturing for Josh to place his Barney figure next to the Barney on the table.
>
> Josh: Places Barney next to Barney.
>
> Instructor: "Right," and then picks up the other, matching Barney figurine and hands it back to Josh. "Match Barney."
>
> Josh: Matches Barney without a prompt.
>
> Instructor: Blows bubbles for Josh.

When you're teaching matching skills, don't allow the child to play with the items you're working with. If you think Josh is incapable of placing the Barney match next to the Barney on the table without fiddling with it first, you'll want to choose other items to match, or you could use pictures instead of the figurines. The same procedure is used for matching pictures as well as 3D items. Once Josh becomes an expert at matching pictures to pictures and real items to real items, you can mix things up by having him match pictures to real items. This is especially important if you plan to use any type of picture schedule in your program.

Puzzle skills can be a fun part of your program, since many children with autism are very visually oriented and puzzles can serve as an effective reinforcer. A child's obsession to finish a puzzle or to put it together in a special order can work to your advantage by encouraging manding for the item or puzzle pieces. Here again, you'll want to bombard your child with language while he's completing the puzzles.

If your child is one of the minority who does not like puzzles you can still work on this skill by carefully pairing the puzzles with strong reinforcers. You can try keeping the television on and have the child move a puzzle piece even slightly in the correct direction so it falls into the correct spot, where you deliver additional reinforcement. Backward chaining is also quite effective. An example of this is where you'd give your child a puzzle that is put together except for one piece, and then have the child complete the task. Once he successfully completes the puzzle with only one piece missing, leave two pieces out of the puzzle the next time.

When you're ready to work on puzzle skills, buy puzzles meant for younger children, such as those with household items, or with farm animals. You can hand your child the pig piece of the puzzle and say "Pig, pig, pig." Then the child can put the pig in its place on the puzzle with or without your help.

Here's an example of how you'd teach Connor to complete a pet puzzle with all the pieces in place, except for the dog:

> Instructor: Hands Connor a puzzle piece with a dog on it and says, "Dog, dog, dog," while prompting him to put the dog piece in the correct spot.
>
> Connor: Puts the dog in, with the prompt.
>
> Instructor: Removes dog piece and hands it back to him, saying "Good...dog, dog, dog."
>
> Connor: Puts dog piece in the puzzle with no prompt.

Building receptive, imitation, and visual performance skills early in Verbal Behavior programming will have a wonderfully positive effect on your child's behavior. These skills, when worked on frequently, will increase your child's compliance, improve your ability to prompt and to practice prompt fading, and very often improve your child's language skills.

The next chapter will show you how to teach your child each of the different verbal operants, and you'll see that the basic procedure of each operant is the same as those shown in this chapter. The difference, though, is prompting. Since you cannot force a child to speak, it's important that you work on skills where you can prompt, and your child can have success, so that he will learn how he will receive reinforcement. This will give him incentive to comply with skills that are more difficult.

In addition, working on these skills will help you become a better Verbal Behavior teacher, working on your prompting and prompt fading skills until you are fluent and can see your own success.

Feel free to come back to this chapter if you need a little reinforcement of your own.

CHAPTER 9

Teaching Verbal Operants

The most important hurdles that you'll have to work on are making sure that your child is well paired with his instructor(s) and that he can mand for several items that are in view.

Once you've reached those milestones, it is time to begin teaching the other verbal operants: tacting, echoic, and intraverbal skills.

Although important, the nonverbal operants discussed in Chapter 8 should not be the focus of your program. Getting your child to communicate either vocally or with sign language or another system as quickly as possible is your goal.

Make sure that Verbal Behavior (VB) intensive teaching sessions include lots of opportunities for the child to practice giving verbal responses, instead of relying heavily on the nonverbal operants that hallmark standard Applied Behavior Analysis (ABA) programs.

The reason nonverbal operants are stressed in ABA/DTT (Discrete Trail Teaching) programs is because they are easier to prompt and can be taught to non-vocal children, while reinforcing success. When I consult with home or school programs and evaluate planned programming and intensive teaching sessions, I am looking for a good mix of all the verbal operants, even with children who are not yet vocal. I want to see at least 50 percent of all the trials include verbal responses (sign or spoken language are both okay). It is harder to teach the verbal operants, but if you keep your eye on your goal—a child who can communicate—you'll see that the extra work is worth it.

You've already learned how to teach manding skills. Your child should be able to mand for several items before moving on to the other operants. The manding must also occur without a verbal model or a prompt to sign. Much too often I see therapists rushing into teaching the other operants before a child can mand, and that's all too often a recipe for disaster.

The child must have manding skills because you will teach many of the initial tacts, echoics, and intraverbals within the "mand frame." That means you'll be using the mands that the child has mastered and transfer those skills to other verbal operants. If your child is not able to say or sign a word when he is clearly motivated to have an item, you won't be able to teach him to tact the item or to master an echoic, either. Manding should always come first.

Teaching Tacting Skills

A "tact" is a label of something you see, hear, smell, taste, or touch. The antecedent for a tact is some form of stimulus (the actual item, a picture, a sound, or a smell) and the consequence for a tact is indirect reinforcement, such as praise.

Technically, the antecedent for a "pure" tact will not include an instructor's question, "What is it?" It should come from the child noticing something in his environment and commenting on it. "Look, there's a cow!" or, "I smell bacon." This spontaneous, pure tact is usually a mand for your attention and that's an area in which children with autism are usually extremely deficient. Manding for attention will come much later in your program. So it is unrealistic to expect to teach tacting without asking the question, "What is it?"

Another reason instructors facilitate tacting in this way is that a stimulus change in the environment is useful to us in creating many opportunities for teaching. Some children with autism will require hundreds of teaching trials per item before they master the skill. A typical child may pick up a new vocabulary word after hearing it just one time, but this is usually not the case with children with autism.

So, simply, this is why the antecedent for a tact will include both the stimulus (the picture or sound, for example) and a question from the instructor (What is it? What do you hear?).

This is only one instance where using Verbal Behavior is not black and white. There will be many times when a child or an adult will say something and you'll realize that it's part mand and part tact. Or part tact, and part intraverbal. Don't worry too much about that, since your goal is to get the child communicating. In reality, most language is "multiply controlled," meaning more than one operant is involved. We capitalize on this during intensive teaching by mixing operants and transferring control from one to another.

Tacting does include labeling what you see, but also what you smell, hear, taste, and touch. This chapter will explain how to teach a child to tact visual and auditory stimuli.

Begin with tacting what you see, followed by what you hear in the environment (animal noises are targeted here, too). Tacting a smell, or how something tastes or feels, is abstract and taught later. Other advanced tacting skills include colors, features (the screen of a computer), adjectives (hot versus cold), and prepositions (the train is on the track versus the train is off the track). Don't think at all about these advanced skills right now. You won't need to get to them until your child can tact hundreds of simple items.

I've seen children newly diagnosed with autism label things such as a yellow chair, or call a fire engine "red." They are taught by well-meaning parents and professionals to label colors, features, functions, and even prepositions before a solid base is established. If you teach colors and more advanced skills too early it will lead to confusion, odd language groupings, and problems with conditional discrimination.

If you teach a child to label "yellow chair," or teach him to say, "The fire engine is red," he might begin to identify all chairs as yellow or call all fire trucks red. It is far better to get children solid with basic tacts and then eventually teach them colors. Only after your child learns these concepts separately and fluently should you even attempt to combine color and the tact. Think of language building as a pyramid, making sure you have a solid base before adding another story.

Remember if you ask your child, "What is it?" and hold up a chair, the answer should be "chair." And if you hold up that same chair and ask "What color?" the answer should be "yellow." The answer "Yellow chair" in response to either of these questions is a significant error that needs to be corrected. Unless your child has 100 or more simple tacts mastered, avoid having him tact colors, features, and other abstract concepts.

Once your child has mastered the basics, you will continue in the same manner with the more advanced skills. The techniques for teaching tacts will be similar regardless of the stimulus.

Okay, you know that your child can now mand for ten items that are in sight. Gather together items that your child sees as reinforcers (and can mand for) as well as pictures of all the items your child has mastered as mands.

The technique for transferring a mand to a tact will work better if you use pictures of the reinforcers, since having the actual items there will create the potential for motivation, meaning that your child will mand for an item, instead of tacting. If your child likes a certain type of candy and mands for it when it is in sight, he will likely do that, instead of tacting. Teaching the child to tact the picture of the reinforcing item after he mands for the actual item is usually more successful.

It's also easier to work with pictures when you're doing a mixed VB session. Storing 100 pictures of items is simply easier than storing the items. Make sure to have some of the actual items, though, as it is more functional for the child to tact a real shoe and real cup instead of just being able to tact photos of those items. Some children will generalize very easily and when taught to tact a picture of a cup will be able to tact several different cups in the natural environment, but others will need specific instruction on not only the difference between a real cup and a picture of a cup, but also different types of cups. Keep these things in mind as you work with your child's tacting skills, so that you can create your program accordingly.

As with all the operants, you're going to need to complete cold probes to assess which items your child can tact with or without prompts. If your child has been able to tact several pictures of reinforcing items and common items at times, create a list of all those words and then test which items your child can tact. Put a plus next to words he can tact, and a minus next to the words where he errors or produces no response at all. You can consider the words with a plus already mastered tacts, so you won't need to probe or teach these tacts.

It's not uncommon to see children new to VB programming with no tacting skills. If that describes your child, look at his mastered mands list for potential targets. Use words that your child can mand for (cookie, swing, cat, milk, top) and use those words across all the verbal and non-verbal operants. Tacting is usually more difficult than the nonverbal operants for most children with autism to master, so make sure you make it a habit to always probe tacting first. You don't want to say "Touch cookie" as a probe for a receptive target and then try to probe a tact by saying, "What is it?" because you've already given the child a prompt that the item is a cookie.

Here's an example of a tacting probe for Ryan:

Instructor: Holds up a picture of a cookie (the cookie should resemble a brand Ryan knows and mands for) and says, "What is it?"

Ryan: Signs "Cookie."

Instructor: "Great job" while blowing bubbles (a preferred item/known reinforcer) and records a "Yes" on a cold probe sheet.

Instructor: Holds up a picture of Ryan's swing and says "What's this?"

Ryan: Signs "Jump" (error).

Instructor: Puts Ryan's hand down and holds up the picture of the swing again and says, "What's this?" immediately moving his hands to prompt him to sign "swing," while saying "Swing."

Ryan: Signs "Swing" with full prompt.

Instructor: "Right, what's this?" holding up the picture of the swing again.

Ryan: Signs "Swing."

Instructor: "Right, it's a swing!" while signing "Swing." Records "No" on the probe sheet.

To record a "YES" on the cold probe data sheet, the child must respond within three seconds and must not chain any other response in with the correct response. He cannot self-correct and get credit for a correct tact. If he is using sign language the answer must be equally as clear. Scrolling through various words—even if they include the correct tact—is counted as a "NO" on the probe sheet.

In the above example with Ryan, the instructor needed to do an error correction before she recorded the "NO" on the probe sheet because even during a probe, errors need to be corrected. If Ryan were vocal the only difference on the probe sheet would be that Ryan must say the correct word instead of signing it. Error correction would also be the same.

The targets that the child gets wrong during the probe should be taught during the teaching session. Ryan, in this case, would need more instruction on tacting the picture of the swing.

John is a vocal six-year-old. The two reinforcers that have been targeted are car and juice. He can say both of these words and can mand for them when they are in sight. Pictures have been taken of both items to aid in transferring the mand to a tact.

> Instructor: Has a real car and real juice present as well as pictures of both of these items.
>
> John: Mands for the juice by saying "Juice" and reaching for it.
>
> Instructor: Holds up a picture of juice and says, "What is it?...Juice."
>
> John: Echoes "Juice."
>
> Instructor: "Right...what is it?" while still holding up the picture of juice.
>
> John: "Juice."
>
> Instructor: Hands John juice as reinforcement.

Some therapists have success using the child's mastered mands and transferring skills from "match to sample" to the tact. Early learners who use sign language do particularly well with this because the instructor is able to pair the word with the sign. The instructor hands them a picture and, once they match a highly preferred item, picture to picture, the instructor then holds up only one of the pictures and says, "What is it?" Since just a few seconds previously, the child saw the sign and heard the word, there's a better chance that the child may say or sign the correct response.

Here's an example of what that trial would look like:

> Instructor: Has pictures of candy, swing, and chips on the table. Hands Aaron a picture identical to the candy and says "Candy."
>
> Aaron: Matches candy picture to candy picture.
>
> Instructor: Picks up the top picture of candy and says, "What is it?"
>
> Aaron: Says "Candy."

You might also try a transfer procedure from receptive to tact. This has proved to be very helpful to Lucas and was the focus of my research and 2005 publication in *The Analysis of Verbal Behavior*.

Here's how that transfer would look:

Instructor: Has pictures of a truck, an oven, and toothpaste on a table, says, "Touch oven."

Sam: Touches picture of the oven.

Instructor: Picks up the picture of the oven and says, "What is it?"

Sam: "Oven."

You'll continue to teach tacting in this manner until your child can tact all the items for which he can also mand, and then you'll begin to teach him common items that are not reinforcing using the same transfer and prompting procedures.

Teaching Echoic Skills

Teaching a child to imitate what you say will often open up the floodgates of language. A child who can and will echo has a much better chance of responding to an echoic prompt and often provides a bridge to transferring skills across operants.

The antecedent for an echoic is *only* a verbal stimulus, so to get a true echoic response, the actual item or picture cannot be present. To assess your child's skills, you will say, "Say ball" when no ball is present.

If your child does not have this skill, he will need systematic instruction to develop it. This is the same process as with all the operants, with prompting, prompt fading, and error correction. The goal will be a true echoic response, but for beginning learners, it's best to begin teaching within the "mand frame." In fact, you've probably already had some success getting your child to echo your words when he's manding for reinforcement.

You don't want to sit your child down and do echoic drills with no reinforcing items present because it will likely cause problem behaviors and work aversion. Instead, use transfer procedures to help your child learn this skill.

Here's an example of an echoic transfer:

Instructor: Has bubbles ready.

Abby: "Bubble" (a mand).

Instructor: Blows bubbles while saying, "Bubble...bubble...say bubble," while hiding the bubble container under the table or out of sight, if possible. Then flash and hold up the bubble container and if Abby has no immediate response model "bubble" again.

Abby: Echoes "bubble" after instructor says "bubble" (with the bubble container hidden).

You may also do another transfer procedure with flashcards of non-reinforcing items by beginning with the child echoing with a picture of an item, and then turning the card over and attempting the echo skill again, without any visual stimulus.

Echoing ability will likely improve articulation, especially if your child can be positioned so that he is looking full at your face, and is able to watch your mouth. Slow down your words or chunk the sounds of the words while exaggerating your facial movements as this may help improve articulation as well.

Teaching Intraverbal Skills

The last verbal operant you'll be learning how to teach is the intraverbal operant. This operant is the ability to answer a question—which is essential for conversation. Many parents of children with autism, including me, long to have their child converse with them. Now I know that it's really not a magical process, but rather it takes systematic procedures to build conversational skills. I really do believe that one day Lucas will have a real conversation with me. We already do have short mini-conversations, since he can answer simple questions, but Lucas still needs instruction on how to ask and answer "WH questions" (questions using who, which, why, when, where).

Here's an example of a typical adult conversation, with operants shown:

Anne: I've never seen you here before (tact/mand for attention). Are you new to the area (mand for information)?

Jayme: Yes, I recently moved here from New Jersey (intraverbal).

Anne: Oh, what part of New Jersey (mand for information)?

Jayme: Ventnor—it's near Atlantic City (intraverbal).

Anne: I love Atlantic City (intraverbal/mand for attention)!

Jayme: Do you like to gamble (mand for information)?

Anne: Yes (intraverbal)!

As you can see, a typical conversation involves a mixture of three verbal operants. Advanced tacts or comments are usually mands for attention and often serve as conversation starters. These can include statements such as, "I love your shirt," or, "It's a beautiful day. The weather is perfect." The second part of conversations are mands for information, asking things like, "Where do you live?" "How do you get there?" and, "Why did you do that?" These advanced manding skills need explicit instruction for children with autism and are taught much later, perhaps months or even years after your child can officially mand for items and actions.

The last part of a conversation is intraverbal responses (answers to the WH questions).

The antecedent for an intraverbal is a verbal stimulus only, but unlike the echoic operant which expects the learner to say the same word as the instructor, the intraverbal response requires a complete different set of words than those contained in the instructor's cue.

It may sound a bit confusing, but actually teaching beginning intraverbal skills are often easy because it involves simple fill-ins to fun activities such as nursery rhymes and songs. As I mentioned previously, my husband stumbled upon Lucas's ability to complete the last word of several sentences in a few songs when Lucas was just two years old. I've also assessed many children and gotten them to complete fill-ins during the assessment, even though parents reported that their children were unable to do so.

To begin teaching intraverbal skills, pick songs with which the child is familiar and hears often. The "I Love You" *Barney* theme song works like a charm for young children. "Old MacDonald Had a Farm" is also a good choice especially for children who are minimally vocal, because filling in "O" after you sing "E, I, E, I" or singing the animal sounds such as "ba" or "moo" are usually easy responses.

Teaching intraverbal fill-ins can also be a functional skill and practiced throughout the day because many day-care settings and preschool classrooms contain activities where these songs will be sung often. Prayers, the Pledge of Allegiance, and popular songs can also be taught in a similar manner to older children and adults.

If your child is vocal, pick an intraverbal fill-in that requires a word that you know the child can say. It's best to begin by choosing a song that the child loves and is motivating for him. Begin by singing the song—"The Wheels on the Bus", for instance—slowly and clearly with some animation, then leave the last word silent for a second or two such as: "The wheels on the _____." If the child doesn't respond, you sing the word and overemphasize it as much as possible. Then attempt singing the song again.

Here's how Nathan learned this skill:

> Instructor: "The wheels on the ___ (two-second pause)...BUS!"
>
> Nathan: Sits and smiles.
>
> Instructor: "The wheels on the B___."
>
> Nathan: "Bus."
>
> Instructor: "Excellent saying bus...Let's try it one more time...The wheels on the ___."
>
> Nathan: "Bus."
>
> Instructor: "Go round and ___ (two-second pause) ROUND!"

Pick only two or three target words for each song you sing. For instance you might have the targets of *bus* and *round* for this song, and then *you* and *me* for the *Barney* "I Love You" song. In both of these songs, the target words come up frequently and most children enjoy singing them. Once Nathan masters all four targets, pick a few additional words from these songs, or introduce new songs.

Once the child masters the last word to several lines from many songs, start backward chaining and leave off the last two words from the sentence. If Nathan masters "star" when you sing "Twinkle, Twinkle, Little _____" your next target would be the phrase "little star."

Don't hold out for more than two or three seconds for a fill-in, since you will be unable to make your child say the words. If this technique doesn't work, you can try holding up a toy star or a picture of a star as a prompt, and then use a tact to intraverbal transfer.

Here's an example of how that would look:

> Instructor: Holds up a picture of a star. "What's this?"
>
> Nathan: "Star."

Instructor: "Right." Puts star down. "Twinkle, twinkle, little ___" holds up star and sings "STAR" loudly. "Let's try that again. Twinkle, twinkle little ___" holds up the picture of the star.

Nathan: "Star."

Instructor: "Great saying star…Twinkle, twinkle little ___." No picture is shown.

Nathan: "Star."

Instructor: "How I wonder what you are…"

The same process works for nursery rhymes (Jack and Jill went up the ___ or Winnie the ___) or for fun or common activities (jump on the ___, wash your ___). Using fill-ins through the day can help embed the language while keeping it very playful. Children using sign language will benefit most if you use signs they already know (their mastered mands). If the child can sign "ball" when he wants to play with a ball, one early intraverbal fill-in could be the phrase, "Bounce on the ___." Or if they like bubbles, you might say, "Blow some ___" and let the child sign the word "bubbles."

You are probably wondering how this all transfers into meaningful conversation. It doesn't right away. This is the starting point. Once your child can sing phrases of songs and has the fill-in technique fairly well mastered, you can bump things up to another level. Look at the mastered tact list to come up with the next intraverbals.

The tact list should have already have dozens of known tacts including bed, cat, pencil, and pizza, so start with these tacts to work on features or functions. You will use these tacts to work on teaching the features, functions, or class using descriptive statements that end with the noun you've targeted. You'd say, "You sleep in a ___" and the child should respond "bed," or "Meow, meow, says the ___" and expect the response "cat."

When beginning this advanced phase, use nouns that can be prompted with a picture. This is important because while it's easy to prompt the statement, "Something you write with is a ___" with the picture of a pencil, it's much too difficult to prompt the phrase, "A pencil is something you use to ___."

Most children won't be able to answer WH questions such as, "Where do you sleep?" until they can fill in the blank to this question ("You sleep in a _____."). Once your child is completing simple fill-ins, you can begin to fade out the visual prompts and then transfer this skill to a more difficult WH question later.

Here are a few examples of transferring from a simple fill-in to have Colin answer a WH question. To be a true intraverbal the response must not be prompted by any visual cues.

> Instructor: "You sleep in a _____."
>
> Colin: "Bed."
>
> Instructor: "Right…Where do you sleep?"
>
> Colin: "Bed."
>
> Instructor: "You drink from a _____."
>
> Colin: "Cup."
>
> Instructor: "Right…What do you drink from?"
>
> Colin: "Cup."

Please make sure that you're working only with words your child can tact fluently; for example, if you child can't tact the word "car," you'll likely get a confused or no response to your question, "Something with wheels is a _____."

I learned this lesson the hard way with Lucas a few years ago when he was taught to answer the question, "What has wings?" with the response "Airplane." Months later I realized that we made a programming mistake when I pointed out real airplane wings and asked Lucas what parts they were, as he was unable to label the wings.

There's simply no point in having your child memorize phrases that have little meaning to him and aren't functional in his world. So make sure to teach him to tact the item as well as relevant features of items before having him learn to answer intraverbal questions without the items present.

I was also in a classroom once where the students were asked to fill in the blank in the phrase, "Something with bristles is…" and the answer was supposed to be "Broom."

Not only could the students not tact bristles when shown a real broom, but there were very few typical children who could tact bristles.

If you're working with a ten-year-old who is on par with a three-year-old in language development, pick tacts and intraverbals that are appropriate for a preschooler. Make sure you keep practicing the tact too, while you're working on intraverbal responses, otherwise the tact may fall apart. If you start to hear your child begin to call a cat "Meow" or a picture of a pizza "Eat pizza" then you know that some of the tacts weren't strong enough. It would be a good idea at this time to hold the intraverbal targets that are weakening the tacts and to go back and get the simple tacts fluent.

Higher intraverbal skills, such as the ability to answer the question, "What did you do last weekend?" or "What did you do at school today?" are more much complex and difficult to teach. I can offer a few pointers if your child gets to this level.

1.   Don't ask questions that you don't know the answers to. Coordinate with your child's teacher to come up with a way to know what your child did in school that day, and you can supply prompts, if needed.

2.   Once your child has mastered all the basic intraverbal skills, practice these high-level intraverbal skills by using some favorite DVDs or books. Pause the DVD or close the book and ask a few WH questions, such as, "Where's Woody?" or, "What's he doing?"

3.   The key to teaching high tacting and intraverbal skills that I learned from Dr. Carbone's clinic is to hold back on direct prompting. You want the child to begin to do some problem solving and give flexible answers. So, if Woody is under the bed in the movie *Toy Story* and your child gives no response or says, "I don't know" to the question, "Where's Woody?" you would not prompt, "Under the bed." Instead you might point to the bed and say, "What's this?" and your child would say "Bed" and you'd say, "That's right, so where is Woody?" while pointing to his location under the bed. After the child can successfully answer your questions with a video on, it is time to have them answer intraverbal questions with no visual stimuli present. This skill is particularly difficult. Don't even

attempt teaching high tacting and intraverbal skills until your child is very fluent with prepositions and can tact all items, actions, and characters in the movie or book before trying activities like this.

Now you know the basics of a Verbal Behavior program. It's time to put it all together into a plan devised just for your child.

CHAPTER 10

Putting It All Together

Now that you know the principles of Applied Behavior Analysis (ABA) and Verbal Behavior (VB), you'll be able to put together a program specifically for your child (if you are a parent) or all of your learners (if you are a professional).

As with all the chapters in this book, I recommend a slow and easy approach incorporating these techniques into your daily life (your natural environment) and then starting intensive teaching sessions.

Implementing ABA/VB Within the Natural Environment

One of the biggest complaints that I hear from parents is that they don't want to get heavily involved in their child's therapy. I hear them say, "I just want to be a parent. I don't want to be my child's therapist or teacher." Teaching, I tell them, is what *all* parenting is about. A parent is a typical child's first and best teacher, and that's even more true for parents of children with autism or other significant impairments. Those children simply don't learn well without explicit instruction, so there really is no way for you to take a backseat and be "just a parent."

Our children will need hundreds of repetitions and they need error correction procedures done throughout the day—not just when they are in a teaching session. If errors or problem behaviors are reinforced in any way, they will go up and your child will not progress. Consistency of your program is essential for your child to learn.

This is why, when asked how many hours per day a child should receive ABA/VB programming my answer is always "during most or all of his waking hours."

Don't panic! This doesn't mean you need to hire someone to come into your home 24 hours a day and have your child in the therapy room or at a table 100 hours a week, but it does mean that you will need to spend a good chunk of time each week doing intensive teaching sessions. Equally important, though, is that every parent and caregiver understands the principles of ABA and VB, so that even a trip to the grocery store can be a learning experience. It can be just as important therapy as they would receive from a behavioral therapist or a speech pathologist.

There is a specific type of teaching called Natural Environment Teaching (NET) that is a contrived and planned exercise and includes data collection—it just happens in the child's natural environment, not in the therapy room. Incorporating VB in the natural environment is a little different in that it's something that occurs on a day-to-day basis as your child goes about his life. You'll need both NET and Intensive Trial Teaching (ITT) in your program.

First you can set up a household where VB is incorporated into your daily living.

These strategies can be used by all adults working with the learner who has a developmental disorder or a significant language impairment. The more consistency everyone who works with the child shows, the better the learner will do. You'll need to explain your strategies to everyone in your child's life: parents, grandparents, babysitters, therapists, and teachers.

These concepts have been explained more fully in previous chapters in this book, but here's the list of things to keep in mind:

1. Be more positive with your child. Use eight positives to each negative or constructive piece of feedback.

2. Reduce demands by giving directions that are easy, that can be prompted, and that you are willing to follow through on.

3. Always be gentle with the child. Don't yell or use physical force to gain compliance.

4. Limit the use of your child's name, especially when placing a demand or saying no.

5. Start identifying potential reinforcers, and make sure to label them two or three times, each time they are delivered to your

child. (You'll do this vocally, or vocally plus signing, if your child is not yet vocal.)

6. Label things throughout the day with one- or two-word phrases in a slightly emphasized, slower, and more animated tone. ("Up, up, up," as you are climbing the stairs with your child.)

7. Do not respond to problem behaviors by withdrawing requests, or allowing the child to gain access to reinforcers while problem behavior is occurring. Teach your child that problem behaviors do not get him what he's seeking.

8. Correct errors, prompt, and do transfer trials throughout the day. Whenever you prompt your child to give an answer, or if you have to correct something he said, make sure to ask him the question a second time to get a more independent response.

Begin implementing these eight suggestions throughout your day. You will likely see a change in your child very quickly. You should also start to feel better about things, too, as you see your child become happier and more compliant. These eight suggestions are a great place to start because they require *no* data collection or documentation, but all are solidly supported by decades of ABA research.

If you can find ways to incorporate these strategies into your daily life, you'll be on your way to incorporating a behavioral approach to teaching your child.

Starting Therapy Sessions

You might be a parent who wants to commit to one hour a day of intensive teaching, a behavioral therapist who is hired to "do VB" for three hours a day, or a speech therapist who sees a child once a week for 30 minutes. In all of these cases, you're going to need some guidance for setting up your intensive teaching session before you feel comfortable jumping in with a VB approach.

First, you'll need to see where the child is in his overall functioning. You should start getting this information by completing the Verbal Behavior assessment form (see Appendix 2) as well as by determining what types of items and activities the child considers reinforcing.

Whenever possible, enlist the help of everyone who works with the child, to thoroughly assess current functioning and to determine potential reinforcers.

After that data have been collected, you'll begin to pair yourself with reinforcing items and activities. Go slowly. Think of yourself as a grandmother spoiling a child, not a bulldozer going in to force learning. (Refer to Chapter 4 if you need to review pairing strategies.)

The first problem likely to come up when you first attempt teaching is problem behavior. This is to be expected because the majority of children beginning these programs have difficulty manding, so they communicate with their physical behavior. Take some data on assessing and treating problem behavior (refer to Chapter 2 if necessary) and put together a behavior intervention plan. During your VB sessions you will continue to keep track of problem behaviors and implement the strategies explained in Chapter 2 to reduce problem behaviors. If you are consistently seeing problem behaviors during your VB sessions, consider consulting with a Board Certified Behavior Analyst (BCBA) who may be able to guide you in these techniques. These assessments of behaviors will be ongoing as new problem behaviors might crop up as you go along.

In addition to implementing strategies to deal with problem behaviors, you will begin a manding program. Manding is thoroughly covered in Chapter 5, but there are some additional tips you'll need to know to incorporate manding trials into a VB program. You'll need to create hundreds of opportunities for your child to mand throughout his day. And make sure that the child has no idea that he's working, by easing in your demands slowly. Manding should not, however, be done during ITT sessions. It should be taught during NET.

What exactly does that mean? Verbal Behavior consultants actually have a bit of disagreement on this, but I believe that as long as motivation is present during the session, it can be considered NET, even if it occurs at the therapy table (where ITT usually occurs). Manding by its very nature occurs within the NET since it involves motivation.

ITT sessions are more easily recognized as they are usually done at the table and are fast-paced, mixed and varied with clear targets, data collection, and some sort of VR schedule of reinforcement. But ITT sessions can also occur on the floor, outside at a picnic table, or at the kitchen counter, as long as the teaching style fits the criteria. Strong reinforcers need to be in place during ITT sessions, and they are usually delivered by the instructor without the child manding.

Children in a VB program need both types of teaching, although the ratio may vary. When you're beginning a program with your child, nearly all of your teaching will be NET, but this is difficult for older children who are in school, because so much of that learning takes place in a non-play environment. If the child is at a table for much of his learning, please make sure that his therapists and/or teachers have lots of reinforcers that can be delivered at the table. You don't want a child who constantly leaves the table to try to go to his reinforcement. I recommend having a small TV/DVD or VCR at the work table. That, coupled with other items, edibles, and activities, can make the table very reinforcing. Remember that you want the child to run happily to the work area— wherever and whatever that is.

NET is planned and purposeful, and involves capturing and contriving motivation. It includes getting the child to mand, and having the child fill in simple intraverbals and practice generalized tacting. If you have a Play-Doh activity, the child can mand for you to open the can. Then you can make a snake with the Play-Doh and your child can tact "snake." Finally, you can have your child fill in the blank: "Hissss, hissssss, goes the _____."

NET is, for most therapists I've trained, more difficult to do, especially if they aren't fluent with the foundations of VB. Even though the teaching is play-based, you still need to be precise. Creativity is essential, because if you get out the same Play-Doh and make the same snake every day, your child will likely get bored and start to respond in a rote fashion.

NET activities will also include some motivation and a VR schedule of reinforcement. Good NET looks like an adult and a child having fun and playing. But, if your child is used to playing with her dollhouse alone and you plop down next to her and start placing demands and asking questions, your presence could be aversive. This will backfire extensively as the dollhouse will lose its reinforcer status, too.

Intensive Teaching Sessions

The picture most people have in their head of Verbal Behavior therapy is that it's a fast-paced intensive teaching session. While this is true, you can only do ITT when you've completely digested the basics of the VB approach. If you try to conduct ITT sessions without background information on both ABA and VB, it will be difficult if not impossible to perform ITT correctly.

Intensive teaching is important. Our children will need lots and lots of it every day in order to make significant gains. While it's possible to do your own ITT, this is the area where—if at all possible—you'd want to put your financial resources. This area of the Verbal Behavior approach needs to be individualized and updated as your child makes progress.

Starting Intensive Teaching Sessions

First, figure out how much time your child needs to be at a table doing ITT during the day (if any). When Lucas switched from the Lovaas/ABA program to a VB program in 2000, he was already comfortable spending almost all of his work time at a table. He had been in preschool for two years at that point and had good sitting behavior and actually liked sitting at the table to do work.

Prior to implementing ITT, make sure that the table you'll be using is paired well with reinforcers. Get the TV/DVD set up and have your other reinforcers within reach. As you're working on pairing the table with reinforcement, you can begin to work on receptive, imitation, and visual performance tasks within your ITT sessions. Some children will require you to leave the television or music on while they are completing a puzzle so that they won't feel that the fun is over and demands will follow. Very few children are comfortable when the reinforcers are abruptly removed and demands presented.

Gradually turn off the television while handing him candy, then turn the TV back on. Then turn the TV off and have him mand for a movie. Then turn the TV back on. Then turn off the TV and have him do one simple imitation skill. Then turn the TV back on.

By doing this you'll eventually be able to increase your VR and begin actual ITT sessions.

To appropriately do ITT you will need to be very organized (with targets, materials, and data sheets) and you must become proficient at "in the chair skills."

Organizing targets, data, and materials is the easier step since these can be done at night when the child is sleeping (or before the child arrives to your office, if you are a professional).

Here's how to get organized:

Step 1

Start putting together your program, by assessing your child. Without assessment you won't know what materials, targets, or documentation forms you will need. The Verbal Behavior assessment form (Appendix 2) will help you with this.

It's important, while doing your assessment, that you keep some sort of documentation of what your child knows and does not know by keeping a skill tracking sheet (see Appendix 4) for each program you'll implement. Do the assessment and the tracking simultaneously. It's not uncommon for me to consult on a program and the therapist has recorded on the Assessment of Basic Language and Learning Skills (ABLLS) that a child has 50 tacts, but there is no record of what they can tact and what they can't tact. Document those details as you assess and you'll find putting a program together much easier.

I recommend completing a separate skill tracking sheet for each of these skills and put an "M" (for mastered) in the date columns required to indicate that this was a previously mastered skill. This sheet should also list skills that are not yet mastered that you will use to aid you in selecting targets. These skill tracking sheets should be kept in a three-ring-binder with tabs so you can easily find the receptive programs, the tacting area, the intraverbal skills, etc. This VB binder should also include a copy of the assessment form, the reinforcer assessment, behavior data, and the old probe sheets.

Here's an example of some of the programs that I would recommend for an early learner just starting a VB program. Each of these would have a separate skill tracking sheet completed:

Receptive directions (clap hands)

Receptive body parts (touch head)

Receptive identification (touch cow)

Toy imitation (roll car back and forth)

Motor imitation (do this…clap hands—don't say "clap hands")

3D matching (3D to 3D…pig)

2D matching (2D to 2D…candy)

Tacting (make three columns, 3D, 2D, and generalized to three pictures)

Echoic (say "ball")

Intraverbal fill-ins (twinkle, twinkle little _____)

Step 2

Select two to three targets for each program and write these targets on the weekly probe sheet (see Appendix 5 for example). I recommend keeping the weekly probe sheet as well as any other daily data (the mand tally sheet, Table 5.1, and your ABC data, Table 2.1) on a clipboard. This way you'll have easy access to it throughout the day. As you select your first targets you will indicate the date that these targets were started on your skill tracking form.

Step 3

I have worked with a variety of different organizational systems and I find the best way to stay organized is a card system. If you start the system early in your programming and keep up with it by adding a card every time a target is mastered, it should work for you, too. When you're starting, write all of the child's known skills on separate index cards. Some consultants recommend using a different colored index card for each of the operants. All of the receptive directions, including receptive body parts, would be written on pink cards, imitation skills on green cards, and all the intraverbal skills on purple cards. If it's easier when you're starting to just use white cards and color code them later using different colored dots in the right-hand corner of the card, that's fine, too.

The card system is important because, as your child acquires skills, it becomes impossible to keep all the mastered items in your head. This means that your child may not practice some skills and you may fall into using known distractors such as, "Touch your head" and, "Where's your nose?" while it's more advantageous for the child to practice more difficult skills such as, "You sleep in a _____."

That skill is much more complex and will lead to other skills such as, "Tell me a piece of furniture" or, "Tell me something soft."

Picture flashcards are used for simple tacting and are easy to keep organized and have ready. The picture does the prompting, so the instructor just gives the direction, "What is it?"

Other skills, such as "Clap hands" and "Do this" (while raising both arms above head) are more likely to be practiced if the mastered skills are kept on index cards. Write only one skill on each card (see Table 10.1). Tacting 3D objects will be easier, too, as the instructor may have a real TV in the room, and a tacting index card with the cue, "What is it?" (real TV).

Table 10.1 Sample Targets for Index Cards in Known Box		
Touch your nose	Clap your hands	Say "banana"
What's this? (EAR)	What's your address? 123 Main Street	Do this (Clap hands)
What am I doing? (Knocking)	The Wheels on the (BUS)	Twinkle Twinkle Little (STAR)

Place your whole card system for your known responses into a plastic recipe or shoe box along with pictures that your child can tact, and mark this box "known."

Then, write each target (two to three unknown skills from each program) on its own index card. Put your target skills on an index card that's a different color from your known skills, and keep the acquisition index cards in a similar but separate box.

Keep all of these materials in a clear rolling bin, and mark the drawers and materials clearly so that any therapist who knows how to do Verbal Behavior programming could sit down and work with your program. Even if you are your child's primary teacher, it's likely that your child will have more than one therapist conducting the sessions, and the more organized you can be, the better.

Step 4

Targets will be mastered on a weekly basis and you have to keep track of that. For most children, a skill is considered mastered once your child has gotten three consecutive Yes's on the cold probe. As soon as that occurs, highlight the item on the probe sheet to indicate the child has mastered the target (see Appendix 5 for a sample weekly probe sheet). Then update the skill tracking sheet and write the date acquired next to the item. Last, place the mastered target onto a known index card and place it in the "known" box. Each week you will rewrite the target probes sheet since you'll be able to take off the mastered targets and add new ones to the mix.

Spend a few minutes each day organizing your materials and you'll be much happier for it. In addition, take an hour (or less) every Friday afternoon or Monday morning to rewrite the probe sheets, select new targets, and gather new materials.

Now that you're organized, teaching will be smoother and you can work on "in the chair skills."

As your ITT sessions begin, they will look like mand sessions with a few easy demands being presented intermittently. Complete probe sheets on the targets you plan to use, even if your ITT sessions are held in the natural environment. You can complete probe data while the child is on the swing, in the sandbox, or even while you're eating lunch.

Ease in more demands and raise the child's VR so that more demands will be made before the child receives reinforcement. Don't go too fast, though. If you do, you'll know pretty soon as behavior problems will likely spike during the sessions.

Mixing Easy and Hard Items

Okay, I've said many times to start easy and make few demands, but what exactly does that mean? Start with your known box. Pull out a pile of knowns and then another pile of unknowns and incorporate them into your sessions. Use the known words first and then occasionally toss in some trial unknowns for the targeted skills. With all new targets, start with a zero-second prompt and then a transfer trial, reducing your prompt as much as possible. The percentage of easy to hard can be anywhere from 80 to 20 or 50/50. More important than the percentages, though, is that the Variable Ratio (VR) schedule of reinforcements be kept very low.

Mixing and Varying Operants

Intensive teaching sessions should include a fluid mix of the different verbal and nonverbal operants (with the exception of matching skills). You can start with a demand to, "Touch your nose" and then have a few pictures already laid on the table and ask the child to, "Touch the truck," then you might touch the picture of the chair and say, "What's that?" Finally you might end the run with an imitation skill that involves a model prompt and then an independent response followed by reinforcement.

Fast-Paced Instruction

What's most striking to people watching a VB session is how quickly it moves. A skilled VB therapist conducting a session with an intermediate learner whose VR is ten should have as many as 20 or 25 responses per minute. Combining fast-paced instruction with mixing and varying targets, as well as monitoring your easy-to-hard mix, plus preventing and correcting all errors appropriately seems like an impossible task, but I assure you, it is not. You will learn to do it, if you practice.

To get good at combining it all, practice the child's program with the child's known cards and target or unknown cards with someone experienced in VB standing nearby and offering criticism. If you don't know anyone like that, a team of two or three motivated people such as your child's caregivers and therapists can watch each other and offer feedback until you're very good at the process.

Here's how a typical five-minute session of intensive teaching run-throughs may look with a skilled Verbal Behavior therapist at the helm. Each run-through is separated by small periods of reinforcement.

Megan's VR is set at five, which means there should be an average of five demands placed in between reinforcement (transfer trials to prevent or correct errors are counted as one trial). The target skills for this session are tacting car and shoe, imitating clap hands and raise arms, and fill in the word "star" for Twinkle, Twinkle, Little ___. The remainder of the skills are known items for Megan.

The instructor's demands are in lower case, while Megan's responses are all caps.

Run-through 1

What is it? ...CUP (known).

What's this? BUBBLES (known).

Good, what's this? Shoe (zero-second prompted trial). SHOE (correct response with prompt). Right, what's this? (transfer trial, no prompt). SHOE (correct response no prompt, reinforcement of candy and praise is given after three correct responses).

Run-through 2

Let's sing... Twinkle, twinkle, little sstt___ (zero-second partial verbal prompt). STAR (correct response with prompt). Great, let's try that again... Twinkle, Twinkle, Little _____ (transfer trial, no prompt) STAR.

Awesome! What's this? BED (known skill).

What's this? SHOE. Great, here's some bubbles (reinforcement delivered after four correct responses).

Run-through 3

Say ball. BALL (known echoic).

What's this? CHAIR (known).

Do this (claps hands and then prompts Megan at her elbows) CLAPS HANDS (correct with a partial physical prompt). Good— clap hands. CLAPS HANDS (transfer trial, no prompt) CLAPS HANDS (correct no prompt).

What's this? CANDY (known).

Say cat. CAT (known echoic).

Do this (while clapping hands). CLAPS HANDS (correct after distracters). Megan receives her reinforcement of 30 seconds of *SpongeBob* video, after six correct responses).

Run-through 4

What's this? C_____? (zero-second verbal prompt) CAR (correct with a partial prompt). Right...What's this? TRUCK (error on transfer trial). What's this? Car (repeat question with a full verbal prompt). CAR (correct with a full verbal prompt). Right. What's this? Ca ___? (transfer trial with a partial verbal prompt). CAR (correct with partial verbal prompt).

Do this (while clapping hands). CLAPS HANDS (no prompt).

Great, do this (while putting arms above head and immediately prompts with a full physical prompt). ARMS ABOVE HEAD (correct with a zero-second prompt). Good, do this (while putting arms above head). ARMS ABOVE HEAD (correct, no prompt).

Great...Do this (while clapping hands). CLAPS HANDS.

Awesome (turns on *SpongeBob* video for reinforcement after four correct responses).

To calculate the VR during this five-minute session you'd add together the number of correct responses at the end of each run-through and then divide by the four run-throughs. In this case that would be three plus four plus six plus four, which equals 17. That, divided by 4, is 4.2. Don't worry that the VR isn't exactly five as this is just one small portion of the session. Calculating the VR once in a while will make sure that you keep on track. I once observed a session where 25 demands were given before reinforcement, while the VR was supposed to be 7. So, have another adult monitor you (or videotape yourself) so you can keep track of your numbers once in a while. You want to make sure you are not way off with your VR so take some time to take data on this.

When you begin, do *not* worry about speed. First, deal correctly with errors and work on your prompting and fading skills before you work on the more complex ITT skills here. Remember that when you first learned to drive a car or play the guitar you had to think about each movement and felt awkward or slow. If you were, in fact, driving a car, you wouldn't want to go 70 mph before you knew the location of all the controls on the car and that you could use them well. ITT is the same. Your speed will increase as you practice and get feedback from observers.

Proficiency doesn't insulate you from errors, either. Don't put too much pressure on yourself to have perfect ITT skills as these skills need to be developed. So, set realistic goals for yourself and, when in doubt, practice your skills with another adult who is acting as your child, video-tape your sessions, and analyze your errors later.

Your skills will improve and so will your child's.

Now that you have, I hope, learned how to begin to incorporate an ABA/VB program to increase your child's language skills and reduce problem behavior, we will now move on to using a behavioral approach to improve your child's self-help skills, such at toileting and dressing.

CHAPTER 11

Teaching Toileting and Other Important Self-Help Skills

Language delays aren't the only issues that concern parents of children with developmental delays. Children with delays lack or are slow to master most self-care skills such as toileting and dressing. It's possible though, using the same skills you've learned for helping your child to communicate, to teach your child these vital skills.

Teaching Toileting Skills

Any parent of any toddler can tell you why toilet training is necessary. This becomes even more obvious as a child ages out of the toddler years without this skill. Wetting and soiling results in the use of a significant amount of time, energy, and resources. Paying for diapers and wipes for three years is expensive enough for typical children, but some of the students with whom I've consulted are as old as 12 and still not toilet trained. That expense can be crippling, especially when that money would be better spent on the child's language and academic needs. In addition, swim diapers and disposable diapers are often difficult to find for older children, and changing their diapers is time lost from working on other vital skills.

Finally—and possibly most importantly—a lack of toilet training always impacts school placement options and access to child care. Typical preschools usually require that a child be toilet trained before he enters the classroom. Many children are denied access to regular schools or certain classrooms because they simply aren't toilet trained when they are young. The situation becomes even bleaker as the child gets older.

These children also find it difficult to be accepted in social situations and a child older than four or five years who isn't toilet trained could easily be ostracized by typical peers if an accident or bowel movement occurs while in public. This often affects the whole family as the child's siblings could be embarrassed by this, too.

Experts have long said that people with autism are among the most difficult to toilet train because many traditional potty training techniques simply don't work for them. While I agree that it's difficult to teach children with autism these skills, it's not impossible. In the classic 1974 book *Toilet Training in Less Than a Day*, by Drs Nathan Azrin and Richard Foxx, it's suggested that by age five, even severely retarded individuals with IQs of 30 can be successfully trained.

There are many other books on this subject, but none that deals specifically with the use of a behavioral approach to train children with autism. I have put together a program for toilet training these children using a mix of techniques from six different books on the subject including three of my favorites: *Toilet Training in Less Than a Day*, referenced above, *Toilet Training Persons with Developmental Disabilities* by Foxx and Azrin (1973), and *Toilet Training for Children with Severe Handicaps* (1984) by Dunlap, Koegel and Koegel (available for under $5 by calling 304-696-2332).

First, you must determine if your child is ready to take on this task. Don't consider just the child's chronological age, but also his developmental age. If your child is three, but has a developmental age of 18 months, it is likely too soon. However, if your child is five, and functioning on an 18-month level, it's probably time to begin. Other questions you need to answer are: Does your child seem to notice or indicate when diapers are wet or soiled? Does your child show interest in the bathroom toilet, hand washing or dressing? Does your child move away from you or hide to have a bowel movement? And finally, does your child have regular bowel movements with no soiling of his diaper overnight? If you answered yes to most of these questions, your child is most likely ready to be toilet trained.

Timing of the instruction is important, too. Don't jump in with toilet training if your child has just been diagnosed since language training, specifically teaching your child to mand, should always come first. Once you establish a good positive behavior program, without any negative reinforcement or consequences, it may be time to start potty training.

Also, don't begin training if your family is planning on moving, you're expecting a new baby, or there are any big changes coming soon for your family. Toilet training is difficult for any child when it is done during stressful times. There is often some backsliding if toilet training is started at inopportune times.

The best time to begin is a time when you know that you'll be committed to the task at hand and will be able to follow through to its conclusion. You will need at least two solid weeks of time to be home a lot to work on this skill and be able to be committed to working almost solely on potty training. Then look at the following three months and make sure that no big changes are planned. I've seen many families have "false starts" with their toilet training because they didn't commit enough time when they began. Once you start a program, you've got to keep going. If you're finding it hard (and it is hard) it will only get harder in a year or two.

If you're not ready to start a formal toilet training program with your child, there are some steps you can take ahead of time that will help when you are ready to begin his program. First, change your child frequently, so that he is always dry. Buy a small potty chair or a potty ring that sits on the toilet (for children aged three and under). If your child is older or larger in size, just use the regular toilet. Each morning and at bath time, sit your child on the potty or potty chair and see what happens. Some children will need lots of rewards for just sitting on the potty, so have reinforcers ready. Look at it as if you are pairing the potty with reinforcement. If you get lucky and your child urinates or has a bowel movement, you reward that behavior like crazy! If you are training a boy, always have him sit on the potty to urinate. You don't want to encourage a boy to stand to urinate until he is fully bowel trained. Bowel training sometimes just happens "by accident" when a child is used to sitting on a toilet. Some children with autism will be able to master urinating standing up, by watching their fathers—but then they never really learn about sitting on the toilet for a bowel movement.

Now is the time to choose words that you want to use to describe the body functions. It may seem silly to consult with your child's babysitter or teacher to decide which words to use, but you must all be consistent. When selecting the words, consider that you'll use these words for a long time, so you might want to use "bathroom" instead of "potty," or "pee" instead of "wee wee" or "tinkle."

Finally, before you start officially, you should identify and document when your child urinates or has a bowel movement for a few days, since most children have patterns that are easy to follow. The body also has reflexes (the ortho colic and the gastro colic) that create the atmosphere for a bowel movement about 15 minutes after getting up in the morning or 15 minutes after eating. Write down when your child eats and wakes up and see if there is a pattern there.

Daytime Bladder Training

If you are ready to begin toilet training in earnest, begin with daytime bladder training. Some children will urinate if placed on a toilet, but show no indication that they have to go prior to that. They'll have accidents if the schedule is stopped. This is completely normal. Being schedule-trained is the first step to be mastered. Create a written toileting plan so that team members, including the teacher, child care provider, and parents, will all be on the same page with regard to the schedule, the reinforcers, the consequences for accidents, and the plan for documentation.

As part of your toileting plan, you should select reinforcers that are immediate, tangible, and motivating. Don't use long-term reinforcers in this instance. Children with autism are not usually motivated by a statement such as, "I'll buy you a train set when you go pee on the potty for one week."

Sometimes a sticker chart can be successful. In this case, the child would place a sticker on a chart for each successful bathroom trip and then after a predetermined number of stickers, the child earns a toy or special treat. If you aren't sure if your child would respond well to this type of token system, don't use it. Instead, select reinforcers that are immediate.

As with all areas of Applied Behavior Analysis (ABA), reinforcers are a powerful tool for you to use. Simply saying "Good job" will not be enough to make it worthwhile for your child to discard the diapers. If you've already got an ABA/Verbal Behavior (VB) program in place, choose a special reinforcer that is used just for toileting. You could use a certain type of candy or a particular video. One child I worked with had access to a folding umbrella as his reinforcer, as the staff reported that he loved rainy days because everyone brought umbrellas into the classroom and the child enjoyed spinning the umbrella over his head. Since toileting is a difficult task, choose an item or activity that the child is crazy for, but doesn't get frequently.

I recommend that everyone who is toilet training their child go to the dollar store and choose items and put them in the "potty bag" from which the child can pick one when he's had a successful time in the bathroom. You should start by reinforcing and allowing the child to pick from the potty bag each time he has a toileting success but then may be able to fade the reinforcement by allowing him to pick at the end of a successful day or week.

When you begin to toilet train your child, leave him in underpants. It's been my experience that regular diapers as well as training elastic band diapers actually hinder the process because they don't allow the child to feel wet and prevent you from detecting accidents promptly.

Ideally, you'll be at home when you begin toilet training, so your child can wear underwear with no pants over them so you can spot accidents quickly. If your child must wear pants on top of his underwear, make sure they have an elasticized waist with no buttons, snaps, or belts. If your child goes to school or if you need to go to a restaurant or a store, put a training diaper or plastic pants over your child's underwear so that he'll still feel wet if he begins to urinate.

If, for whatever reason, you want to routinely put your child in diapers during training, you can purchase a potty alarm which slips inside the diaper and alerts you and the child when he is wet. These alarms are commercially available at www.thepottystore.com. Continue to use diapers for naps and nighttime sleep, as this type of bladder control comes much later. But don't put the diaper on two hours before bedtime, as you don't want your child to have an excuse to urinate in the diaper. Take the diaper off immediately when your child wakes, too, and sit him immediately on the toilet, as this is the time when your child will have the best chance of a successful trip to the toilet.

After your child has used the potty (even if he was unsuccessful) make sure to have him wipe himself correctly, pull up his own pants, and wash his hands with help if needed. Teach your child to pull his pants down to his ankles, but not to remove them completely, as completely undressing can be a difficult habit to break. Encourage your child to be as independent as possible with the entire toileting process.

There are five basic steps to formal toilet training, as described in several books on the subject, including *Toilet Training in Less Than a Day* and *Toilet Training for Children with Severe Handicaps.*

They are:

1. *Extra drinks:* The child should be given salty foods and extra drinks (eight to ten glasses per day) to allow for many toileting possibilities. Make sure your child drinks these liquids consistently throughout the day, such as four ounces an hour, so that his need to use the bathroom will be more predictable. Giving your child 20 ounces here and there will cause his need to use the toilet to be too varied.

2. *Schedule toileting:* This should happen at least once or twice an hour. Tell the child, "Time to go potty" (or whatever word you're using). Have him say, or sign, "potty" and take him. The child should be heavily reinforced if he urinates or has a bowel movement (BM) at this time. Once the child starts initiating trips to the bathroom, you can stop using the schedule.

3. *Dry pants checks:* There are two purposes for this. One is to allow for detection of accidents and the other is an opportunity to reward your child for having dry pants. Ask the child, "Are your pants dry?" and have him feel the outside of his underwear. These dry pants checks can be done at intervals of five minutes to an hour depending on your child's level of success. Dry pants should be rewarded with a reinforcer. If you notice an accident, do a dry pants check immediately.

4. *Positive practice for accidents:* Toileting experts such as Dr. Richard Foxx suggest that "positive practice" is a very important step in the toilet training process. Positive practice means that you'll take your child quickly from the spot of the accident to the toilet and back again five to ten times in a row.

5. *Data recording:* Keep a record of all successful trips to the potty as well as urine or BM accidents. This will help indicate the length of time between urination as well as the usual time

your child has a BM. Keeping data will help you measure the success of your program.

I do believe that some children can be toilet trained successfully without the need for positive practice although it has been an effective procedure for many, including Lucas. Positive practice is actually a form of over-correction and, in many cases, serves as an effective punisher. Don't use it in the beginning of your toilet training program, though. First, see if placing the child on a schedule and using positive reinforcement will work without any negative consequences such as positive practice. If the child is large or combative or if the child is in a school situation where the repetitive punishing action would be too stigmatizing, you may not be able to use any form of positive practice.

In your toileting plan, make sure to spell out exactly what procedures you'll be using, and alter that plan as needed. Make sure that everyone is doing the same procedures and is consistent. If you choose not to use positive practice, make sure you are calm, but firm and matter-of-fact, when your child has accidents. Do not laugh, or smile or make your child think that you were pleased in any way. Prompt the child to change his clothes, but give him no unnecessary attention.

Other Techniques to Try

Picture schedules may be successful for some children so that they know when a trip to the bathroom is coming in their schedule. If you do use a picture schedule, make sure that you have an additional picture of a toilet on it, so that the child may request a trip to the toilet outside of the schedule.

If your child has limited awareness, he can be taught to lean forward while on the toilet, or give him gentle pressure to the lower abdomen to help with toileting.

Children who stand or squat to have a BM in their diapers will find a step stool under their feet while sitting on the toilet to be helpful. This also is a good idea to use with children whose feet do not yet touch the floor when sitting on the toilet.

Other children may respond well to wearing underwear with their favorite characters on it since they won't want to get the character wet. If your child doesn't care what underwear he puts on, stick with cheap white underwear that can be bleached or tossed away without too much worry.

A timer is a tool to use if your child spends too much time sitting on the toilet. A child shouldn't sit for more than five minutes without starting to have a bowel movement or urinating.

You also need to create a relaxing environment in the bathroom. If your child is having problem behaviors when it's time to use the bathroom, it probably means that the room is not well paired with reinforcement. If that's the case you will need to take a step back and reward the child heavily for entering the bathroom and sitting on the toilet at scheduled intervals.

Bowel Training

A child who is bladder trained may begin to spontaneously have BMs in the toilet at the same time he urinates. (This is why it's essential for boys to sit on the toilet until they are fully bowel trained.) The child who has a BM in the toilet—whether intentionally or spontaneously—should be given an extreme amount of reinforcement because the child will not be wearing diapers or pull-ups during bowel training, and BMs can be quite messy.

If BM accidents continue to occur after bladder training is firmly established, take a look at your reinforcement and make sure it's as strong as it can be. Use your child's most coveted reinforcers for bowel training and it should go easier. However, if all else fails, consider implementing positive practice by cleaning up your child in the normal manner and then taking him back and forth from the toilet to the spot of the accident five to ten times in a row.

We used positive practice when we bladder trained Lucas at 4½ years of age. Within a month or two, Lucas was schedule trained for urination, and we were thrilled. But he still continued to have BMs in his underwear every day or every other day. He would wait until I was not looking and go behind the sofa, squat and have a bowel movement in his underwear. Needless to say, I was very frustrated.

After three or four months of this, with no change, I called Dr. Richard Foxx on the telephone because I had met him on previous occasions and hoped he'd be able to help with my dilemma with Lucas. He recommended that I find a reinforcer that Lucas would "die for" and that we begin using positive practice for the bowel accidents.

So, on those occasions that Lucas did have a BM in the toilet I put him in the car and took him through the McDonald's drive-through, telling him the entire time how proud I was that he pooped in the potty. I only had to use positive practice one or two times because within two days of my speaking with Dr. Foxx, Lucas was completely trained for both bowel and bladder.

Nighttime Training

After your child is fully daytime trained for both bowel and bladder, you can work on nighttime training. If you're lucky, your child will train himself, and will begin to wake up dry each morning.

After five mornings of waking up with a dry diaper, allow your child to sleep in underwear. You should expect an occasional accident at night, but getting rid of the diapers is a necessary step.

If you're not one of those lucky parents whose child wakes up dry each morning without additional intervention, there are several strategies you can implement. Encourage liquid consumption in the afternoon and then limit it to just small sips of liquid within two hours of bedtime. Make sure your child has a regular bedtime and wake time, too. This is a particularly difficult step for children with autism who don't sleep well, so if your child does wake during the night, make sure that they use the toilet immediately.

If nighttime wetting persists, check with your child's doctor to make sure that everything is physically all right. Do not scold, shame, or punish nighttime accidents, since your child has no control over his bladder when he's asleep. If your child is over ten years old and still having nighttime accidents, and you've ruled out a medical problem, consider using a potty alarm and consulting with a toileting expert.

Teaching a Child to Initiate Bathroom Use

Unfortunately, many people stop their toilet training when their child is successful with scheduled trips to the bathroom. This means that the child doesn't learn to initiate his own use of the toilet without prompts. If you have to ask the child if he has to go potty every hour or so, he is not fully toilet trained so your work is not done.

As with all ABA/VB programs, you can help your child become more independent and master this skill by fading the schedule and other prompts, with careful planning. If your child uses signs or pictures, you can (while he's on the schedule) prompt the child to sign "toilet" to you, or if he's verbal, to say "Toilet" or "Bathroom" or whatever word you've chosen when you say, "It's time to go potty."

As you're on the way to the bathroom, stop the child two or three times, shrug your shoulders in a playful way and ask the child again, "Where do you have to go?" Have him respond by signing or saying potty. You're practicing having him mand for the toilet, and each time he is successful manding for the toilet (with or without a prompt), make sure to reinforce the behavior.

As soon as your child is successful with urinating on the toilet on a schedule of once an hour and has not had an accident for two or three days, increase the schedule to every 90 minutes. Remember to use a timer for this because different caregivers may not know when the child last visited the toilet. Again, once the child is dry for two or three days, increase the schedule to every two hours. If you see an increase in accidents when you add time to the schedule, you can increase the interval more gradually.

Your child will need to feel the urge to urinate if he's going to initiate bathroom trips, so the interval will have to be elongated to accommodate that need. During training, make sure to have the child always tell you when he needs to use a bathroom because, when you're out of the house, the child will need you to help him find a bathroom.

Dealing with Accidents After Training is Complete

An occasional accident happens with most children and is nothing to worry about. However, if your child has more than an occasional accident, you need to immediately begin investigating the cause, to halt backsliding.

Rule out medical problems, such as a stomach virus or urinary tract infection, first. Dietary changes can also cause accidents to increase if your child is eating more junk food or just eating more in general. Both medication and supplement changes can also cause bowel and bladder accidents.

Remember to check in with your child's teacher to see how the toileting is going at school too. If the child can initiate bathroom trips at home, in school, and in the community, they should never be placed on any sort of toileting schedule. Toilet scheduling occurs when children are placed in a new school or classroom where it is routine for all the students to go to the bathroom upon arriving at the school, at snack time, lunch time, and before dismissal. A fully trained child in this environment will stop practicing initiation skills because they won't have the urge to urinate. He may begin to have accidents because his stomach is upset or he just drank two boxes of juice at lunch, and needs to use the bathroom outside the schedule. The child in this case is now prompt dependent because he was placed on a toileting schedule after he was toilet trained.

Likewise, don't ask your child, "Do you need to use the potty?" throughout the day. Instead ask your child that question in a similar pattern as you would a typical child—perhaps before a long car ride or going swimming.

If you discover in your investigation that your child is having accidents for no apparent reason, at similar times each day, put him back on a schedule for those parts of the day.

We had an issue with Lucas last summer where he had a handful of bowel accidents while he was swimming in the pool. In this case we had him wear underwear under his bathing suit to serve as a sort of barrier and then we decided we would toilet him according to a schedule when we went swimming only. We had him sit on the toilet before getting his bathing suit on over the top of his underwear and then we'd take him out of the pool every hour and toilet him before allowing him to re-enter the pool. For the remainder of the day we didn't have him on a schedule or ask him frequently if he needed to use the toilet.

How Long will It Take?

Toilet training depends on your child, just as it does with typical children. It could take days, weeks, or even months, but should not take years. To accomplish successful toilet training, use a data driven, coordinated approach. Whatever you do, don't give up! Revise your plan if you need to, but never throw in the towel. Your child needs this vital skill more than any other skill, and you can help him reach this goal.

Teaching Other Self-Help Skills

Hand washing and dressing skills are also important both in conjunction with toilet training and in general. Self-help skills—anything from washing hands to hanging up a coat in a school cubbie, eating chicken with a fork, or putting on a shirt—are all tasks that need to be taught differently than language skills. These self-help skills are a compilation of multiple skills that are all chained together.

We tried to teach Lucas how to wash his hands for—literally—years! Four years to be exact. We tried verbally prompting him for each step of the sequence and we tried laminating a series of pictures above the sink, but, much to our dismay, Lucas didn't learn to wash his hands until he enrolled in the ABA school when he was six. It turned out that the use of verbal prompts or a series of pictures are not efficient ways to teach complex skills such as hand washing. Instead, these skills are best taught by developing task analysis, physically prompting as much as needed from behind the child and, when possible, reducing your prompts for each step gradually. After giving the direction, "Wash your hands," try not to talk during the procedure since the goal is for the child to complete the steps independently and verbal prompts will be difficult to fade.

At the same time Lucas was learning to wash his hands at school, I was finishing up my ABA coursework and learning about the use of task analysis. Task analysis will be useful for teaching your child any skill that has multiple steps. The best book I've found to help you write task analysis is called *The Pyramid Approach to Education: Lesson Plans for Young Children* by Dr. Andy Bondy and a few of his colleagues (2002).

Create your own task analysis by writing down each step of any complex skill. It's easier if you first watch a typical student doing the skill, or if you do it yourself and write down each step.

Here's an illustration of task analysis for hand washing:

Grasp both knobs and turn the water on.

Put right hand on soap pump and left hand under spout.

Press pump two times.

Rub hands together for five to ten seconds.

Place hands under faucet to remove all soap.

Grasp both knobs and turn water off.

Get towel and dry both hands.

Place towel back on towel rack.

When working on this task with your child continue to use the same type of soap (bar or liquid) and keep it at the same place on the sink so the procedure will be consistent. If you keep the soap dispenser on the left side of the sink, you may want to teach your child to put his right hand under the spout and pump with his left hand. The important thing is that everyone is consistent so your prompts can be faded.

Once the task analysis is in place, assess your child's abilities for each of the different steps. Ask your child to wash his hands and see what he does. Does he turn on the cold water? Just stand there? Does he pump the soap continuously until you tell him to stop? Your assessment will get you to a starting point.

Don't teach each skill separately; teach it as one fluid act. The child needs to get a feel for the whole process together and he needs to memorize the correct order of the process. You can facilitate this by standing behind the child and prompting his arms and hands only as much as is needed to prevent errors and keep the steps going smoothly to their conclusion.

The task analysis is helpful when teaching your child to do chores, too. You can create one for setting the table or even picking up toys. Develop a consistent series of steps that the child can learn, and he will learn them. I worked once with a 14-year-old girl with Down Syndrome who was learning to set the table at school. My first question to the teacher was how she wanted the girl to begin. Should the girl bring over one plate at a time? Four plates at a time? When should she return for utensils or should she pile these on top of the plate before her first trip to the table?

The teacher admitted to me that she hadn't really thought about the process and wanted her to simply "set the table." I explained that she would have to set up a procedure so that she could prompt the student gently from behind and gradually fade out her prompts until the student was independent in this task.

These same procedures can be used for many self-help skills including dressing and undressing. Backward chaining techniques can also be helpful with these skills, where you'd ask your child to perform the last action in the sequence, after you had done the rest. Once that skill is mastered, you'd have the child complete the last two acts.

So, if taking off shoes and socks is the goal, you unlace your child's shoes and loosen them up enough so that when you give the direction, "Take off your shoes," it is simple for the child to comply.

The same is true for removing socks. You can loosen the socks to make them come off very easily, and then you ask your child to complete the task.

When teaching dressing and undressing skills, use larger clothing so there is less effort in pulling on pants or pulling up socks. Remember to physically prompt from behind whenever possible, so that you can feel how much work the child is doing and how you need to change your prompts. In many ways, teaching toileting and self-help skills are just as important as teaching language skills. The use of a behavioral method in these cases also has a scientifically proven track record. The more your child can do for himself, the better his opportunities will be in the future. Independent toileting and self-help skills will also free you up to spend more time focusing on language and academic skills.

CHAPTER 12

Final Thoughts

The previous chapters in this book have given you the tools to put together a Verbal Behavior (VB) program for your child to help him learn to navigate the world. But, as you've probably gathered, setting up the program is actually the easy part. There is no cure for autism as of yet, so autism will remain a fact of life for you, your child, and your family for the foreseeable future.

But it is by no means an irrevocable tragedy. In this chapter I'll be taking off my "Board Certified Behavior Analyst (BCBA) hat," and putting on my "parent hat," in hopes of giving you some advice about coping with a diagnosis and getting appropriate treatment in place as soon as possible.

This chapter will be directed at parents in particular, but I hope that professionals read it as well because working with the family and understanding their emotions is a large part of effectively working clinically with a child.

These are the things I would tell you, if you were my best friend and you'd just found out that your child had a life-changing disability, such as autism or Down Syndrome.

Accept the Diagnosis Immediately

The sooner you realize that your child is disabled, the sooner you will be able to help him or her. Consider that your life is forever changed and will be different than you ever imagined it would be. But never lose hope that your child can have a happy and productive life.

I had a friend tell me early on that once your child is diagnosed with autism, you enter an entirely new world where autism is the center. I found this true in my life, as I began to "date" events as they related to

Lucas's diagnosis. I'd remember that something happened "one year before" the diagnosis or "six months after" therapy began. I know how difficult it is to accept that your life has changed forever, so quickly, but the sooner you can do it, the better. It really is a fact of life that a diagnosis of autism will completely change the dynamics of your family.

However, if you can't immediately accept the changes in your life, you're not alone. I remember when Lucas was diagnosed, a psychologist told me that I needed to grieve because Lucas was not normal and would never be normal, and therefore my life would never be normal. I told her that at that point I wasn't ready to give up on a normal life, that all I was willing to grieve were his preschool years. I couldn't—when he was three—grieve his entire life.

I was convinced then that with intensive therapy, Lucas could recover completely. I needed to stay optimistic but my husband Charles took a different route. On the way home from the developmental pediatrician's office where we had just been given Lucas's diagnosis, Charles was saying things like, "I guess he'll never get married or go to college," "He'll have to live with us forever," etc. In tears, I told him to be quiet, that I wasn't going to go there yet. Not that day or not that year. I was not going to begin predicting what Lucas was going to be like 20 years down the road. My first priority was to get him into an intensive Applied Behavior Analysis (ABA) therapy program and take things day by day.

On the day of Lucas's diagnosis, I literally thought of recovery as black and white and even envisioned a "recovery party" for Lucas a few years down the road. I thought Charles was being extremely pessimistic by predicting a poor outcome for Lucas. Our initial reactions were surprisingly very different.

Dealing with the diagnosis of autism often causes this type of reaction in two-parent families. One parent, like me, will be completely optimistic and sometimes unrealistic, and the other parent will have the opposite view. But, in the end, my optimism and Charles's pessimism/realism balanced out as we started to listen to each other's hopes, dreams, and fears for Lucas.

But whatever strides Lucas has made, our lives were indeed changed forever. When he was diagnosed, I was a nurse. Now, seven years later I'm a BCBA and founding president of the Berks County Autism Society. And just in the past few years I have become an author, speaker, consultant, and expert on autism.

Defining Failure

Don't consider yourself or your child a failure if he doesn't "recover" from autism, or if he needs a lot of support in school, or if he never becomes conversational. My friend Carole has a son who also has moderate autism. Carole was my first "autism friend" after someone gave me her phone number and I went to her home to see a therapy session for her son Anthony. In the ensuing years, Carole and I have spent a lot of time together. It was Carole who flew to Florida in 2000 to see Dr. Vincent Carbone and got me started by giving me the first information about VB, and I wonder what my path would have been without her friendship. Yet even with her support and counsel, and my hard work and her hard work, our sons are still far from indistinguishable from their peers. We've discovered in our friendship, that if "curing" autism was just about hard work, our sons would have recovered years ago.

But we also know, through our friendship that ABA and VB have helped our sons to function at their highest possible levels. And, even though they are now ten years old, it's not time to throw in the towel—the learning continues. And so we press on.

Most of the parent-authored books that I've read about autism are written by people whose children have done very well with therapy and some of these parents claim that their child is fully "recovered" from autism. But even with the best, most state-of-the-art ABA program in place, the majority of children with autism will not fully recover. After meeting hundreds of children with autism, I've only met a few children that I would consider to be completely indistinguishable from their peers or "recovered" from autism. For this reason, I feel recovery shouldn't be your primary or only goal.

However, almost all children will significantly improve with behavioral therapy—and your child may recover or become indistinguishable from his peers—and that's reason enough to keep working and keep trying. Some kids will go farther than others, just as some typical children go farther in life. Don't compare your child's path with any other child's. Look instead at your child's strengths and use those to bolster his weaknesses.

Avoid the High-Functioning/Low-Functioning Trap

Sometimes the best thing you can do for your child is to ignore what some people suggest. In the autism community there might be professionals or family members who will try to convince you that your child is too high functioning or low functioning to benefit from ABA or VB. My experience tells me differently. It doesn't matter where your child falls on the spectrum—ABA and VB can help.

I often hear parents say that their child "just" has PDD-NOS (pervasive developmental disorder not otherwise specified) or "I don't want to join that autism support group because my child has Asperger's Syndrome and most of those people have 'low-functioning' kids." Making those comparisons is like comparing different cancers. There may be different outcomes for different types of cancers, but any cancer diagnosis is life-altering.

To be honest, I'm not sure what "high-functioning" autism really is. I used to think Lucas was high functioning because when he was a toddler, he went to a typical preschool and looked "normal." He didn't have stereotypical behavior like hand flapping or rocking. He wasn't aggressive or self-injurious. Yet, he was diagnosed with moderate autism, so I then stopped using the term "high functioning" for him.

Instead, I began to use Lucas as a gauge for other children with autism. With Lucas in the middle, I'd assess other children as either high functioning or low functioning. But then it dawned on me one day that those boxes helped no one. That realization happened when I visited the ABA school that we were considering for Lucas and when I observed circle time, there was one boy who was having a tough time sitting in his chair. He flopped on the floor and was giving the staff a hard time. The teachers had procedures in place to deal with his behavior, but by the time circle time was over, I was shaken.

After that display I was concerned that Lucas was too high functioning for that school. The school director asked me to elaborate on that thought and I explained that with behavior such as that during circle time, I feared that Lucas would be taking a step backwards to be placed in this class.

The director informed me that the child who was disruptive during circle time was able to read chapter books, had math skills at grade level, and had more language than Lucas did.

It was at that moment I decided to throw "high-functioning" and "low functioning" out of my vocabulary. They are very subjective terms and therefore, ultimately useless. If teachers actually had to place their students in a line from highest functioning to lowest functioning, they'd likely have a rough time of it, since different children have skills in different areas. A child could have high academic skills and poor social abilities, or high language skills with problem behavior.

Unfortunately, the more "normal" your child looks, the more you will probably have to advocate for him. Some parents try to keep the diagnosis "quiet" and that may add to the problem because oftentimes it is hard to hide differences from school children. These "high-functioning" students are more likely to be teased or ignored for not fitting in, and they tend not to receive the individualized instruction in language, academic, or social skills that would help them fit in. So, you'll probably have to educate professionals and gently push to make sure your child (who looks typical) gets services he needs.

For all these reasons, I feel very strongly that we shouldn't label children as high functioning or low functioning. Instead, your child's strengths and needs should be assessed and he should receive services to help him improve.

Get as Much Therapy as You Can, as Soon as You Can

When Lucas was first diagnosed, I believed that his case was mild and had every expectation that he'd recover, and not require much treatment. I was wrong, although I didn't know it at the time.

I attended a one-day workshop given by Dr. Glen Dunlap and told him that Lucas probably wouldn't require too much treatment and he told me to treat Lucas's diagnosis like it was the most severe case of autism. He said that in his long experience he'd seen children who were three years old and similar to Lucas who did turn out normal by the time they were eight years old—and others who didn't. Likewise, he'd seen severely autistic children for whom he had little hope of any recovery become indistinguishable from typical children by the time they were eight.

Dr. Dunlap told me that he had seen the mild to moderate kids actually fall behind the severe kids because they didn't get the intensive therapy they so desperately needed. He suggested that I would never regret giving Lucas more therapy than he needed, but I would always regret it if I sat back and did not treat him aggressively enough, based on my own reading of his skills.

It might not be easy to get appropriate services for your child, but it's essential. Don't always take what professionals tell you at face value. I had the mom of a 30-month-old child tell me that her son's speech services had been cut to one hour per month, even though it was clear to me that he was still at least a year delayed. She surmised that he must be doing well or "they" wouldn't have reduced his services. Instead of relying on that opinion, this woman should have looked to her son's standardized language assessment scores and other objective data. Not providing needed therapy, or a premature reduction in services, is much more likely to be due to staffing and funding concerns, than to an improvement in your child's learning. When in doubt, look to objective data to drive your child's needs for intensive intervention.

Be Ready to Advocate for Your Child

Perhaps the most jarring piece of advice I'm going to give you, is to tell you that you are probably going to have to advocate for your child's rights to receive quality education and services. I hope that you are one of the lucky ones who doesn't have to fight (most likely because others have beaten the path for you) but in case you're not, there are ways to make your battles run more smoothly. The best way to prepare for this is to keep very organized records of what your child needs and what services he is receiving.

As soon as Lucas turned three and was diagnosed with autism, I felt like I was fighting for him at every turn. I learned almost immediately that the provision of educational services was going to be very far from ideal, and actually would be completely unacceptable to me. Within months I found myself in a legal battle that lasted two years, with lawyers, court reporters, and witnesses involved. It was amazing to me because— on paper—I had everything on my side. I had a Master's degree, I had worked as a staff development coordinator where I trained nurses how to write good goals, and I had also been a nurse manager, so I was used to keeping good records and being assertive when necessary.

My family was in the area, so I had a lot of local support to watch my children, and I had financial resources, was internet savvy, and had a car to get me places. I also had the ability to obtain private evaluations and learned quickly how to navigate the system.

I believed that I could handle the educational court system, called due process, fairly easily. But again, I was wrong. It was unbelievable to me just how hard I had to fight for Lucas to get what I believed he needed and deserved. It was expensive too, since there are no public defenders for the parents of special needs children.

The county where I lived (like most counties) was at least ten years behind the times and did not provide ABA therapy in the late 1990s. But I believed that my child's life was at stake so I acted quickly. I'm happy to report that with the help of a few friends who also filed for due process at the same time, the educational establishment did move forward, with improved services not only for Lucas, but for every child in the county.

Some people don't want to advocate, and, instead, will pick up and move to a more accessible school district literally "chasing" a good program. In my mind it's better to change the program options in the place where you live as opposed to moving, because services are more often determined by school administrators and school board members who may change at any time. You may move into a district that is very "autism treatment friendly" only to find that a year later a newly elected school board opts to cut funding for those very programs. Or you may sell your house and uproot your whole family only to find out that the outstanding teacher you relocated for has developed a medical problem and is no longer there. Educational policies and programs—whether positive or negative—are not written in stone.

I've chosen to spend my time in the past few years working with my school district, county, and state to develop good systems to meet the needs of all children with autism. Through the Pennsylvania Verbal Behavior Project as well as through private consultation, I have had the privilege of working with hundreds of professionals who are implementing ABA and VB programs within public school classrooms for students with autism. They are seeing first hand that ABA and VB principles do work with children with autism and related disorders. One teacher commented to me recently that she has no idea how she used to teach students with autism in the past. She has been so impressed with all her students' progress since implementing an ABA/VB approach that she recently went on to become a Board Certified Associate Behavior Analyst.

So while you're advocating, please keep in mind that you need to work with your child's school to create appropriate programs. This is not going to happen overnight and will take a lot of work and perseverance on your part. Advocating should never become personal or nasty. Try to be assertive, but never aggressive. You need to keep the bar set high for your child, but realize that you may need to compromise on some points to get your child some important services.

In the United States children with special needs are entitled to Free, Appropriate, Public Education (FAPE). While that sounds good, it doesn't mean that school administrators will be eager to give your child the services that you think constitutes FAPE.

So, be prepared. Keep all your papers in a three-ring binder. This way you'll be able to find your reports easily. You'll also look more organized and will be prepared to address inadequacies in your child's program, if you need to.

Bring a friend or family member to each Individual Education Plan (IEP) meeting or any place your child's education or programming will be discussed. Have them take notes or audiotape the meeting (you need to give the school administrators a few days' notice if you're planning to do this). It really can be intimidating to sit at a meeting like this by yourself, because the "other side of the table" will likely have six or seven people, so it is important to always bring someone with you.

Soliciting the help of an advocate is also a good step you may need to take early on. I found a free advocate from our local mental health association when Lucas was three years old and her advice and support were invaluable. I have also paid advocates and attorneys along the way when I've needed more specific legal information. Your local autism support group may be able to guide you towards reputable advocates and attorneys in your area.

Put things in writing whenever possible too. If you have phone conversations with anyone regarding your child, get their name and address and send a letter to them to confirm the contents of your conversation. You can also follow up on all in-person meetings with a letter documenting what you observed or heard at the meeting, what your concerns are, and what information you still need (and who promised it to you, if applicable).

The 2004 book *How to Compromise with Your School District without Compromising Your Child* by Gary Mayerson (the father of a child with autism) will be helpful to you, as will the website www.wrightslaw.com.

Prepare yourself so you can avoid litigation by learning as much as you can about special education law, and attend advocacy workshops and network with other parents who have experience.

Also remember the principles of ABA when working with professionals or school administrators. Just as when working with your child, you need to pair yourself with reinforcement (bring donuts to a meeting), ease in demands (don't ask for everything at once), and give positive reinforcement when things are going well!

Try One New Treatment at a Time

One of the mistakes that a lot of parents of newly diagnosed children make, is to try several treatments simultaneously. While I completely understand the zeal to begin helping your child as much as possible, in the case of autism, a more pragmatic approach will yield the best results.

Begin implementing an ABA/VB program as soon as possible and see how your child responds. There is an abundance of other treatments available including special diets, medications, biomedical treatments, sensory integration therapy, and relationship-based therapies. If you begin everything simultaneously, you'll have no idea what is working and what is not working.

Dr. James Coplan, the developmental pediatrician who diagnosed Lucas, told me that he did use medication to treat autism, but *only* after a good behavioral program was in place.

For us, Lucas's ABA program worked such wonders that had we started medication at that same time, we would not have known about the dramatic effect caused simply by a good behavioral program.

We have tried a dozen medications over the past seven years, but the vast majority caused negative side effects. We tried each medication separately, so that we'd know its specific effect. One thing that I didn't do but now recommend is to keep a running list of all medication (with dosages), supplements, and other treatments you try. Record the dates different medications were started and stopped and also list all positive and negative side effects while your child was on each medication.

It's also important to know when to stop a treatment, or to add something different to the mix. I've seen teenagers who have been on the gluten–casein free diet for years, while still having major behavior problems because no ABA program is in place. Their parents are so stressed out trying to make sure that their child doesn't eat any wrong foods, that they don't notice the sound research behind behavioral programs such as ABA/VB.

This isn't to say that everyone should ignore non-traditional or biomedical treatments, because they do help many children. It's just that I believe a behavioral program should come first and that all other interventions should be added one at a time so you can evaluate their effects.

Learn All You Can about Your Child's Treatments

When Lucas began his Lovaas ABA therapy program, his consultant recommended that one parent learn how to be a therapist. She recommended that I get a babysitter for Spencer (my typical child) for five hours per week, so that I could conduct a real therapy session with Lucas. For me, this was particularly good advice because I found that I enjoyed it so much that I went on to earn my BCBA certification. But in general it was very helpful to be "in the chair" with Lucas, seeing his responses and noting his strengths and weaknesses. Whenever his consultant visited, I'd work with Lucas and get the consultant's constructive feedback that eventually enabled me to train the other therapists who came into our home.

If you are a professional working with a child who has autism or a related disorder, you need to get the parents involved. Give them reading materials and have them watch you do the therapy. If you're working with a family where the parents have become expert at therapy (a common occurrence in the autism community) then allow them to show you what works for their child. Involve parents as much as possible, since they will be there long after the professionals move on.

Take Care of Yourself and Take It One Day at a Time

Autism and other developmental disabilities can overtake your life if you let them. Everyone comes to the table with their own baggage and issues but there are only so many things you can accomplish in one day.

Involve your extended family and friends as much as possible by bringing them to conferences and therapy sessions. Give them this book to read, so that they will know what you're trying to accomplish with your child. The more they know, the better they'll be able to support you. My mom came to every consultant workshop to learn what she could and she helped me as I founded the Autism Society of Berks. Both my parents were there for me at my due process cases and also watched my children frequently so I could attend conferences and meetings. My sister and other friends were there for me when I needed someone to listen, or when I became frustrated with the diagnosis and the process.

Lean on your friends as much as you can and involve them in every aspect of your programming and in your child's life. Let others care for your child with autism as much as possible, since children with special needs must learn to listen to other people and develop relationships with adults other than their own parents. You need a break too, so when someone offers to take your child for a few hours, take them up on the offer! When feasible, hire a regular babysitter too so you can get regular breaks and not have to rely on an occasional offer of free babysitting from family and friends.

Although autism will be a driving force in your life, it's important that you take lots of side trips to spend time away from the diagnosis. Dr. Coplan told my husband and I to spend time alone, spend time as a couple, and that sometimes my husband and Spencer should do things together and sometimes Lucas and I should spend time together. He also suggested that we occasionally leave Lucas at home and do something as a couple with Spencer, as he felt that we needed to enjoy life and experience things without Lucas occasionally.

Dr. Coplan also told my husband and I to get some marriage counseling on the same day he diagnosed Lucas. When Lucas was first diagnosed, my husband complained to Dr. Coplan that when Lucas requested milk in the middle of the night, I immediately ran to get him milk. My husband said he thought that water would be a better drink in the middle of the night. Dr. Coplan said that if we were having difficulty agreeing on what Lucas's nighttime drink should be, we'd be in for some rough waters when it came time to make the huge decisions about Lucas's future.

My husband and I did seek counseling and found it was a great place to work out our feelings of grief as well as finding common ground in our decisions about Lucas's future. While many couples separate or divorce as a result of their child being diagnosed with autism, I feel our marriage is stronger because of it. We've been forced to get on the same page and make decisions together to help Lucas improve. Several sessions of counseling did get us to the point we are now and I highly recommend individual or couples counseling for anyone who is struggling.

There are also support groups that will offer you help. If there's one in your area that you can attend physically, do it. Online, you can visit www.autism-society.org, or www.autismspeaks.org. I have found support via the internet to be invaluable. Although you may not always find people in your community who share your frustrations, you will almost always find like-minded parents on line who have "been there, done that."

I'm already seeking out parents of older children to guide me through puberty with Lucas. It's also important to make friends with the parents of children who are your child's age so that you can email or call for support when you need to chat, vent, or ask a question that they might be able to answer. You are never alone in this.

Remember to take everything one day at a time. This is not a sprint. It's a long marathon with lots of hills and valleys. You need to pace yourself because you will most likely have years of therapy ahead of you and twists and turns as your child ages. You'll be working with your child on language and then vocational and/or academic skills and then preparing your child to live independently or perhaps even attend college. Remember through each stage that there is always reason to hope and that you are working so hard because you want your child to have the best possible life.

Making Lemonade

My own journey through autism has been about making the best of the situation for myself, my son, and my family.

Ironically, before Lucas was diagnosed, I was at a Moms Club meeting where the icebreaker question was to tell what we had done before our children were born, and what we planned to do in the future. Spencer was only one at the time and Lucas was two and a half and not yet diagnosed with autism. When it was my turn to answer the icebreaker question, I stated that I had been a nurse manager and that in the future I could see myself going back to school and earning a Ph.D., and becoming a researcher, writer, and expert on some (yet to be determined) topic. Although I had no idea that topic would be autism, I am happy to report that I am fulfilling that prediction of more than seven years ago.

So while my life has changed dramatically, I've managed to attain my own goals, while helping Lucas to achieve his.

Along the way I've also discovered how much I love helping all children. I love teaching professionals how to provide better services for our children and teaching parents how to better care for their children. Most of all, I love working with the children who are all so unique and who teach me something new each day. I've been told that I've made lemonade out of lemons, and maybe that's true. But I really do see my life's journey thus far as being very rewarding.

That doesn't mean it's over or that there won't be frustrating challenges ahead for me and Lucas on the steep and slippery slope of autism. But I know that as long as I keep myself focused on my goals to help both my children be the best they can be, I'll find a way to the top of that mountain with my family intact.

Until then, we're living our lives one step at a time, taking time to enjoy the scenery along the way.

Beginning a Verbal Behavior program is your first step. It's time to take that step, and see how far you, your child, and your family can go.

APPENDIX 1

Glossary of Terms/Acronyms

ABA   Applied Behavior Analysis. The science of understanding and improving socially significant behavior.

ABC   Antecedent–Behavior–Consequence. Describes the three-term contingency of all behavior.

> Antecedent   What happens immediately before a behavior. Could be a direction such as "get in line" or it might be an alarm clock ringing.
>
> Behavior   A movement of a living organism that can be observed. Description of what the behavior looks like.
>
> Consequence   What happens immediately following a behavior that either increases or decreases the chance of that behavior happening in the future.
>
> Examples:
>
> A—"Touch nose." B—Touches nose. C— Cookie given.
>
> A—"Do puzzle." B—Says "NO!" C—Task removed.

ABLLS   Acronym for the Assessment of Basic Language and Learning Skills written by Drs James Partington and Mark Sundberg. Is often used within ABA/VB programs as an assessment tool, curriculum guide, and skills tracking system.

Backward chaining   A method of instruction used to teach whole tasks such as building puzzles and singing songs. When using this technique to teach a child to sing a song, you would first leave out one word for the child to produce, for example, "Twinkle, Twinkle, Little ____." Once the child can sing "Star," you can leave out two words to make the child to sing "Little star," and so on.

Baseline   The period of observation where data are collected before any new intervention is started.

BCBA, BCaBA   A BCBA is a person who has satisfied the requirements to become a Board Certified Behavior Analyst. A person with a BCBA holds at least a Master's degree while a Board Certified Associate Behavior Analyst (BCaBA) holds at least a Bachelor's degree. Besides meeting minimum education standards, the BCBA and BCaBA must also complete ABA coursework, be supervised by a current BCBA, and pass a written exam. Information on how to become or locate a BCBA is available on www.BACB.com.

Conditioned reinforcer   A reinforcer that was previously neutral but now has become a reinforcer. Tokens or money are good examples of conditioned reinforcers since they can be used to pay for items.

Deprivation   A reinforcer which is unavailable for a specific period of time will result in an increase in behavior that had obtained these items in the past. We can take advantage of natural states of deprivation by conducting mand sessions before lunch when the child will most likely be more hungry.

Discrete Trial Teaching (DTT)   Three-term contingency (A–B–C) used to teach skills to children with disabilitites. Each separate trial is used to teach a new skill.

Echoic   Repeating what someone else says. Can be immediate or delayed. Identified by B.F. Skinner as a verbal operant.

Edible reinforcers   Food items that may be used during ABA/VB programming. The instructor should always pair food items with praise and other more natural reinforcers so that edibles may eventually be faded.

Errorless teaching   A technique used within VB programs to prevent or reduce errors. A prompt is provided immediately after the direction is given or question is asked and then that prompt is faded out via a transfer trial.

Error correction   This technique is used to correct errors that have not been prevented. The question or direction is re-stated, a prompt is provided, then a transfer trial is used to reduce or eliminate the prompt.

FAPE   An acronym for a Free, Appropriate, Public Education. In the United States under a Federal law, children with disabilities (aged 3–21) are entitled to this level of education.

Imitation skills   Copying someone else's motor movements.

Intensive Trial Teaching (ITT)   This refers to fast-paced VB instruction usually done at the table using errorless teaching, fading in demands, mixing and varying, prompting procedures, and an established VR.

Intraverbal   Filling in blanks or answering WH questions. Responding to someone else's Verbal Behavior with no visual or other stimuli present.

Mand   A request for an item, action, attention, or information.

Matching to Sample   The ability to match items or pictures to identical or similar items or pictures.

Motivational Operation   Referred to as an MO. Basically this is someone's motivation or desire for something, whether that is an item, action, attention, or information. Effected by the principles of satiation and deprivation.

Natural Environment Teaching (NET)   The child's current interest or MO controls the teaching activity. Teaching targets are weaved into play and other fun activities.

Operant   A behavior defined in terms of its antecedent and consequence. For example, the antecedent of a mand is the motivation, and the consequence of a mand is receiving the requested item.

Pairing   The process of using high reinforcers to condition people, materials, and environments to become reinforcing. We want the child running to the work area and to people before placing demands.

PECS   An acronym for the Picture Exchange Communication System developed by Dr. Andy Bondy and Ms. Lori Frost. Using this system, children are taught to exchange pictures of items to indicate their wants and needs.

Probe (cold)   Data collected before any teaching is done for the day to see if the child can respond after several hours of no teaching. Cold probes are usually done first thing in the morning or at the start of first teaching session.

Prompt   A hint or cue to aid the student to make the correct response. A prompt should be part of the antecedent condition and added before the learner has a chance to respond. Whenever you add a prompt, you must be planning how to fade out that prompt so the student can become independent with the response.

Receptive skills   The ability to understand language and follow directions.

Reinforcement   A consequence following a behavior that increases the probability that the behavior will increase in the future. Can be positive or negative.

Satiation   The opposite of deprivation. A reinforcer loses its value because the child has had his fill of it.

Skinner   B.F. Skinner was the founder of the experimental analysis of behavior. He also is the author of the book *Verbal Behavior* (1957).

Tact   Labeling/naming some sensory nonverbal stimuli such as an object, picture, adjective, location, smell, taste, noise, or feeling.

Task analysis   A breakdown of a skill which involves multiple steps used to help identify and teach problematic steps in the sequence.

VR   An acronym for a variable ratio schedule of reinforcement which is the average number of correct reponses in between the delivery of reinforcement.

Verbal Behavior   Any communication involving a listener including speaking, signing, exchanging pictures, pointing, writing, typing, gesturing, etc. Also includes crying or displaying other problem behaviors in an attempt to obtain attention or tangibles, or to escape unwanted activities.

Visual performance   Skills include matching tasks, sorting, puzzle building skills, and block design.

Verbal Behavior Assessment Form

Date of completion ___/___/____ Person completing _____

Child's name _____ Age _____ Date of birth __/__/____

Parent's/guardian's name(s) _____

Sibling(s) name (s) and ages _____

Phone _____Alternate phone _____

Address _____

_____

Email address _____

Medical Information

Diagnosis (if known) _____ Age at diagnosis _____

Does your child currently go to school and/or receive any therapies or special services?   Yes   ☐   No   ☐

If yes, please list name of school or provider, frequency and location of services:

Current medication:

Allergies:

Special diet/restrictions:

Describe eating and drinking patterns. Please indicate if child can feed self, what texture/types of foods he/she eats. Also list if bottle or sippy cups are used:

Describe sleeping patterns:

Describe toileting issues:

Language Information

Does your child ever use any words?   Yes   ☐   No   ☐

If yes, please describe the amount of words and give examples of what he/she says:

If no, does your child babble?   Yes   ☐   No   ☐

If yes, please list sounds you have heard:

Manding Assessment

Can your child ask for things he/she wants with words? Cookie, juice, ball, push me?   Yes   ☐   No   ☐

If yes, please list the items/activities your child requests with words:

If no, how does your child let you know what he/she wants? Circle your answer.

Gestures/pointing/pulling an adult   Sign language   pictures

Crying/grabbing

Tacting Assessment

Can your child label things in a book or on flashcards? If so, please estimate the number of things your child can label and give up to 20 examples:

Echoic Assessment

Can your child imitate words you say? For example if you say "say ball" will he/she say "ball"? Will he/she imitate phrases?; and if you say "I love you" will he/she repeat "I love you"?   Yes ☐   No ☐

Does your child say things he/she has memorized from movies or things he/she has heard you say in the past?   Yes ☐   No ☐

If yes, please describe:

Intraverbal Assessment

Can your child fill in the blanks to songs? For example if you sing "Twinkle, Twinkle Little _____," will your child say "star"?; and if you sing "E, I, E, I ___" will your child fill in "O"?   Yes ☐   No ☐

Please list songs that your child fills in words or phrases to:

Will your child fill in the blanks to fun and/or functional phrases such as filling in "Pooh" when he/she hears "Winnie the _____"?; and will he answer "bed" when he hears "You sleep in a _____"?   Yes ☐   No ☐

Will your child answer WH questions (with no picture or visual clue)? For example if you say "What flies in the sky?" will your child answer "bird" or "plane"?; and will he/she name at least three animals or colors if you ask him/her to?   Yes ☐   No ☐

Receptive Assessment

Does your child respond to his/her name when you call it? Circle your answer.

Almost always   Usually   Sometimes   Almost never

If you tell your child to get his/her shoes or pick up his/her cup, does he/she follow your direction without gestures? Circle your answers.

Almost always   Usually   Sometimes   Almost never

If you tell your child to clap his/her hands or stand up will he/she do it without gestures?

Almost always   Usually   Sometimes   Almost never

Will your child touch his/her body parts if you say "Touch your nose" or "Touch head"?   Yes ☐   No ☐

If yes, please list the body parts he/she will touch without any gestures from you:

Imitation Assessment

Will your child copy your actions with toys if you tell him/her "do this"? For example, if you take a car and roll it back and forth and tell your child "Do this" will your child copy you?   Yes ☐   No ☐

Will your child copy motor movements such as clap hands or stomp feet if you do it and say "Do this"?   Yes ☐   No ☐

Will your child move his/her fingers (fine motor movements) such as putting his/her pointer finger out or his/her thumb up if you do the motion and say "Do this"?   Yes ☐   No ☐

Visual Skill Assessment

Will your child match identical objects to objects, pictures to pictures, and pictures to object if you tell him/her to "match"?

Yes ☐   No ☐   Unsure ☐

Will your child complete age-appropriate puzzles?

Yes ☐   No ☐   Unsure ☐

Behavior Assessment

Is your child currently able to sit at a table or on the floor and do simple tasks with an adult?   Yes ☐   No ☐   Unsure ☐

Please list any problem behaviors (crying, hitting, biting, falling to the ground, making loud noises, hitting his/her own head) that your child displays that you are concerned about. Please estimate the number of times these behaviors happen (100 times/day, ten times/week, one time per day) as well as a few examples of when the behavior occurs. Also describe what strategies you have tried to control these behaviors and whether these strategies have been successful or not:

Please list any additional comments or concerns below:

Sign Language Examples

APPLE

X twists against corner of mouth.

CANDY

Index finger on cheek, twist hand.

COOKIE

Right fingertips touch left palm, twist and touch again (cookie cutter). (see BISCUIT)

CRACKER

Palm-in A taps arm near elbow.

DRINK

Thumb of C-hand on chin, drink from C. (see SIP)

FISH

Palm-left flat hand flutters forward like fish swimming.

MILK

Horizontal C to horizonatal S squeezes in a milking motion: repeat. (can do with 2 hands)

POPCORN

Palm-in S's indexes flick up alternately.

POTATO

Bent 2 fingers tap on back of left S. (see IRELAND)

WATER

Index finger of palm-left W taps chin.

BALL
Claw hands, form ball shape.

BOOK
Palm-to-palm hands open
to palms-up.

CAR
Right C-hand behind left C;
right moves backwards.

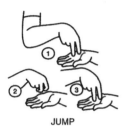

JUMP
V-fingertips stand on left palm, jump up to
bent fingers and down again. (see HOP)

MOVIE
Heel of palm-out 5 rests on side of
palm-in left hand; 5 waves slightly,
side-to-side. (see FILM)

OPEN
B-hands, palms-down and sides
touching, twist apart, palms
facing up.

PUSH
Palm-out flat hads push forward.

PUZZLE
Palm-out index finger jerks back
to an X on forehead.

SWING
Right bent V sits on 2 fingers of
left hand and swings forward and
back. (see TRAPEZE)

TOILET
Palm-out T shakes.

Skills Tracking Sheets

Skills Tracking Sheets – Sample
Child's name: Johnny C.

Criteria: 3 consecutive days "YES" on cold probe

Put an "M" in the date column for each skill already mastered. List skills that are not yet mastered, and insert date introduced and date when the skill was acquired.

Skill: Receptive directions

	Target	Date introduced	Date acquired
1	Clap hands	M	M
2	Arms up	6/5/06	6/10/06
3	Shake head no	6/5/06	6/24/06
4	Shake head yes	6/5/06	6/24/06
5	Stand up	6/24/06	
6	Sit down	6/24/06	
7	Knock on the table	6/30/06	
8			
9			
10			
11			
12			
13			
14			
15			
16			
17			

✓

Child's name: _____

Criteria: consecutive days "YES" on cold probe

Put an "M" in the date column for each skill already mastered. List skills that are not yet mastered, and insert date introduced and date when the skill was acquired.

Skill: _____

	Target	Date introduced	Date acquired
1			
2			
3			
4			
5			
6			
7			
8			
9			
10			
11			
12			
13			
14			
15			
16			
17			
18			
19			
20			

Weekly Probe Sheets

Weekly Probe Sheet – Sample

Select two to three targets from each skill tracking sheet. When you introduce the skill, note the date of introduction and acquisition on the skill tracking sheet.

Child's name: _____Week beginning: _____

	Op.	Target skill	Mon		Tues		Wed		Thur		Fri	
1	Rec.	Clap hands	Yes	No	Yes	No	Yes	No	Yes	No	Yes	No
2	Rec.	Stomp feet	Yes	No	Yes	No	Yes	No	Yes	No	Yes	No
3	Rec.	Stand up	Yes	No	Yes	No	Yes	No	Yes	No	Yes	No
4	Rec.	Touch head	Yes	No	Yes	No	Yes	No	Yes	No	Yes	No
5	Rec.	Where's your belly?	Yes	No	Yes	No	Yes	No	Yes	No	Yes	No
6	Rec.	Touch shoe	Yes	No	Yes	No	Yes	No	Yes	No	Yes	No
7	Rec.	Find cup	Yes	No	Yes	No	Yes	No	Yes	No	Yes	No
8	Rec.	Where's the car?	Yes	No	Yes	No	Yes	No	Yes	No	Yes	No
9	IM	Do this (touch head with both hands)	Yes	No	Yes	No	Yes	No	Yes	No	Yes	No
10	IM	Do this (clap hands)	Yes	No	Yes	No	Yes	No	Yes	No	Yes	No
11	MS	Match candy (picture to picture)	Yes	No	Yes	No	Yes	No	Yes	No	Yes	No
12	MS	Match fish (picture to picture)	Yes	No	Yes	No	Yes	No	Yes	No	Yes	No
13	Tact	What's this? (cookie)	Yes	No	Yes	No	Yes	No	Yes	No	Yes	No
14	Tact	What's this? (swing)	Yes	No	Yes	No	Yes	No	Yes	No	Yes	No
15	Echo	Say "Bubble"	Yes	No	Yes	No	Yes	No	Yes	No	Yes	No
16	Echo	Say "Juice"	Yes	No	Yes	No	Yes	No	Yes	No	Yes	No

	Op.	Target skill	Mon		Tues		Wed		Thur		Fri	
17	IV	Twinkle, Twinkle little _____ (Star)	Yes	No	Yes	No	Yes	No	Yes	No	Yes	No
18	IV	The Wheels on the _____ (Bus)	Yes	No	Yes	No	Yes	No	Yes	No	Yes	No
19			Yes	No	Yes	No	Yes	No	Yes	No	Yes	No
20			Yes	No	Yes	No	Yes	No	Yes	No	Yes	No
21			Yes	No	Yes	No	Yes	No	Yes	No	Yes	No
22			Yes	No	Yes	No	Yes	No	Yes	No	Yes	No
23			Yes	No	Yes	No	Yes	No	Yes	No	Yes	No
24			Yes	No	Yes	No	Yes	No	Yes	No	Yes	No
25			Yes	No	Yes	No	Yes	No	Yes	No	Yes	No
26			Yes	No	Yes	No	Yes	No	Yes	No	Yes	No

Codes:

Rec. = Receptive	IM = Imitation	MS = Match to Sample
Tact = Tact	Echo = Echoic	IV = Intraverbal

Weekly Probe Sheet

Select two to three targets from each skill tracking sheet. When you introduce the skill, note the date of introduction and acquisition on the skill tracking sheet.

Child's name: _____ Week beginning: _____

	Operant	Target skill	Mon		Tues		Wed		Thur		Fri	
1			Yes	No	Yes	No	Yes	No	Yes	No	Yes	No
2			Yes	No	Yes	No	Yes	No	Yes	No	Yes	No
3			Yes	No	Yes	No	Yes	No	Yes	No	Yes	No
4			Yes	No	Yes	No	Yes	No	Yes	No	Yes	No
5			Yes	No	Yes	No	Yes	No	Yes	No	Yes	No
6			Yes	No	Yes	No	Yes	No	Yes	No	Yes	No
7			Yes	No	Yes	No	Yes	No	Yes	No	Yes	No
8			Yes	No	Yes	No	Yes	No	Yes	No	Yes	No
9			Yes	No	Yes	No	Yes	No	Yes	No	Yes	No
10			Yes	No	Yes	No	Yes	No	Yes	No	Yes	No
11			Yes	No	Yes	No	Yes	No	Yes	No	Yes	No
12			Yes	No	Yes	No	Yes	No	Yes	No	Yes	No
13			Yes	No	Yes	No	Yes	No	Yes	No	Yes	No
14			Yes	No	Yes	No	Yes	No	Yes	No	Yes	No
15			Yes	No	Yes	No	Yes	No	Yes	No	Yes	No
16			Yes	No	Yes	No	Yes	No	Yes	No	Yes	No
17			Yes	No	Yes	No	Yes	No	Yes	No	Yes	No
18			Yes	No	Yes	No	Yes	No	Yes	No	Yes	No
19			Yes	No	Yes	No	Yes	No	Yes	No	Yes	No
20			Yes	No	Yes	No	Yes	No	Yes	No	Yes	No
21			Yes	No	Yes	No	Yes	No	Yes	No	Yes	No
22			Yes	No	Yes	No	Yes	No	Yes	No	Yes	No
23			Yes	No	Yes	No	Yes	No	Yes	No	Yes	No
24			Yes	No	Yes	No	Yes	No	Yes	No	Yes	No
25			Yes	No	Yes	No	Yes	No	Yes	No	Yes	No
26			Yes	No	Yes	No	Yes	No	Yes	No	Yes	No

Codes:

Rec. = Receptive	IM = Imitation	MS = Match to Sample
Tact = Tact	Echo = Echoic	IV = Intraverbal

Helpful Websites

www.verbalbehaviorapproach.com: Mary Barbera's website, which contains updated information about the Verbal Behavior approach.

www.verbalbehaviornetwork.com: A website started by Parents of Autistic Children (POAC) in the early 2000s. It's a great place to find out about training sessions and offers sample forms and VB programs.

www.firstsigns.org: Offers a list of milestones typical children should be meeting, in an effort to help with early diagnosis of autism.

www.difflearn.com: A resource for purchasing materials to aid your ABA or VB program, including timers, flashcards, and books.

www.superduperinc.com: A resource for purchasing a wide variety of educational materials for both typical children and children with autism, including reward system prizes.

www.establishingoperationsinc.com: Has consultants who specialize in providing hands-on training workshops and setting up at-home language-based programs for children with language delays and/or autism.

www.lifeprint.com: Offers help with teaching sign language.

www.northernspeechservices.com: Offers information about workshops (online and at conferences) about various issues in teaching speech.

www.talktools.net: Offers information and products to facilitate muscle-based speech therapy.

www.google.com: Search engine useful in finding photos to copy or download to help your VB programs.

www.thepottystore.com: Offers a wide variety of toilet training tools and charts.

www.wrightslaw.com: Offers information about special education law, education law, and advocacy for children with disabilities.

www.autism-society.org: Resource for information and support about autism. Site for the Autism Society of America.

www.autismspeaks.org: Offers support for families with autism, as well as raises funds for research.

www.BACB.com: The Behavior Analyst Certification Board website with information about BCBAs and how to find them in your community.

References
and Further Reading

Azrin, N. and Foxx, R. (1974) *Toilet Training in Less Than a Day.* Champaign, IL: Research Press.

Barbera, M.L. and Kubina, R.M. (2005) "Using Transfer Procedures to Teach Tacts to a Child with Autism." *The Analysis of Verbal Behavior, 21,* 155–161.

Bondy, A., Dickey, K. Black, D. and Buswell, S. (2002) *The Pyramid Approach to Education: Lesson Plans for Young Children,* Volume 1. Newark, DE: PECS.

Bondy, A. and Frost, L. (1994) *The Picture Exchange Communication System.* Newark, DE: Pyramid Educational Products.

Buchanan, S.M. and Weiss, M.J. (2006) *Applied Behavior Analysis and Autism: An Introduction.* Ewing, NJ: COSAC.

Caffrey, T. (2004) Video Presentation—Teaching Verbal Behavior in the Classroom. PA Verbal Behavior Project, October 2004.

Carbone, V. (2004) Practical Applications of Verbal Behavior Research. Autism Society of Berks County—Fifth Annual Conference.

Carbone, V. (2004) The Verbal Behavior Approach to Teaching Children with Autism. (CD modules) Collaborative Training Solutions.

Carbone, V. (2004) Invited Address: Clinical Applications of Verbal Behavior Research with Children with Autism. Presentation at the 30th Annual Convention of the Association of Behavior Analysts: Boston, MA.

Carr, J.E. and Firth, A.M. (2005) "The Verbal Behavior approach to early and intensive behavioral intervention for autism: A Call for Additional Empirical Support." *Journal of Early and Intensive Behavioral Intervention, 2* (1), 18–26.

Carr, E.G. and Kologinsky, E. (1983) "Acquisition of Sign Language by Autistic Children Using a Time Delay Procedure." *Journal of Applied Behavioral Analysis, 16,* 297–314.

Cautilli, J. (2006) "Validation of the Verbal Behavior Package: Old Wine New Bottle—A Reply to Carr and Firth (2005)." *Journal of Speech and Language Pathology—Applied Behavior Analysis, 1*(1), 81–90.

Charlop, M.H., Schreibman, L. and Thibodeau, M.G. (1985) "Increasing Spontaneous Verbal Responding in Autistic Children Using a Time Delay Procedure." *Journal of Applied Behavioral Analysis, 18*, 155–166.

Cooper, J.O., Heron, T.E. and Heward, W.L. (1987) *Applied Behavior Analysis.* Upper Saddle River, NJ: Prentice Hall.

Drash, P.W., High, R.L. and Tudor, R.M. (1999) "Using Mand Training to Establish an Echoic Repertoire in Young Children with Autism." *The Analysis of Verbal Behavior, 16*, 29–44.

Drash, P.W. and Tudor, R.M. (2004) "An Analysis of Autism as a Contingency-shaped Disorder of Verbal Behavior." *The Analysis of Verbal Behavior, 20*, p 5–24.

Drash, P.W. and Tudor, R.M. (2006) "How to Prevent Autism by Teaching At-risk Infants and Toddlers to Talk." *Journal of Verbal Behavior.* Online at www.sarnet.org/lib/Drash.doc, accessed 10 December 2006.

Dunlap, G., Koegel, R. and Koegel, L. (1984) *Toilet Training for Children with Severe Handicaps.* Huntington, WV: Autism Training Center.

Eikeseth, S. (2001) "Recent criticisms of the UCLA Young Autism Project." *Behavioral Interventions, 16*, 249–264.

Engleman, S. and Carnine, D.W. (1982) *Theory of Instruction: Principles and Applications.* New York: Irvinston.

Exkorn, K.S. (2005) *The Autism Sourcebook: Everything You Need to Know about Diagnosis, Treatment, Coping, and Healing.* New York: ReganBooks.

Foxx, R. and Azrin, N. (1973) *Toilet Training Persons with Developmental Disabilities.* Champaign, IL: Research Press.

Gustason, G. and Zawolkow, E. (1993) *Signing Exact English.* Los Alamitos, CA: Modern Signs Press, Inc.

Hall, G.A., and Sundberg, M. L. (1987) "Teaching Mands by Manipulating Conditioned Establishing Operations." *The Analysis of Verbal Behavior, 5*, 41–53.

Harris, S.L. and Weiss, M.J. (1998) *Right from the Start: Behavioral Intervention for Young Children with Autism: A Guide for Parents and Professionals.* Bethesda, MD: Woodbine House, Inc.

Howard, J.S., Sparkman, C.R., Cohen, H.G., Green, G. and Stanislaw, H. (2005) "A Comparison of Intensive Behavior Analytic and Eclectic Treatments for Young Children with Autism." *Research in Developmental Disabilities, 26*, 359–383.

Iwata, B.A., Pace, G.M., Cowdery, G.E. and Miltenberger, R.G. (1994) "Toward a Functional Analysis of Self Injury." *Journal of Applied Behavior Analysis, 27*, 197–209. (Reprinted from *Analysis and Intervention in Developmental Disabilities, 2*, 3–20, 1982)

Jacobson, J.W., Mulick, J.A. and Green, G. (1998) "Cost-benefit Estimates for Early Intensive Behavioral Intervention for Young Children with Autism: General Models and Single State Case". *Behavioral Interventions, 13*, 201–226.

Kates-McElrath, K. and Axelrod, S. (2006) "Behavioral Intervention for Autism: A Distinction Between Two Behavior Analytic Approaches." *The Behavior Analyst Today, 7* (2), 242–252.

Kibbe, H. and Twigg, C. (2001) Teaching Verbal Behavior: Hands On Training for Tutors and Therapists, Workshop #4. Presentation: New Jersey.

Koegel, L.K. and LaZebnik, C. (2004) *Overcoming Autism.* New York: Penguin Group.

Latham, G. (1990) *The Power of Positive Parenting.* North Logan, Utah: PandT Ink.

Lovaas, O.I. (1987) "Behavioral Treatment and Normal Educational and Intellectual Functioning in Young Autistic Children." *Journal of Consulting and Clinical Psychology, 55,* 3–9.

Lovaas, O.I. (2003) *Teaching Individuals with Developmental Delays.* Austin, TX: Pro-Ed.

Lowenkron, B. (2004) "Meaning: A Verbal Behavior Account." *The Analysis of Verbal Behavior, 20,* 77–97.

Manolson, A. (1992) *It Takes Two to Talk: A Parent's Guide to Helping Children Communicate.* Toronto: Hanen Centre.

Maurice, C. (1993) *Let Me Hear Your Voice: A Family's Triumph Over Autism.* New York: Knopf.

Maurice, C., Green, G. and Luce, S.C. (1996) *Behavioral Intervention for Young Children with Autism: A Manual for Parents and Professionals.* Austin, TX: Pro-Ed.

Mayerson, G. (2004) *How to Compromise with Your School District without Compromising Your Child: A Field Guide for Getting Effective Services for Children with Special Needs.* New York: DRL Books.

McEachin, J.J., Smith, T. and Lovaas, O.I. (1993) "Long-term Outcome for Children with Autism who Received Early Intensive Behavioral Treatment." *American Journal of Mental Retardation, 97,* 359–372.

Michael, J. (1985) "Two Kinds of Verbal Behavior plus a Possible Third." *The Analysis of Verbal Behavior, 3,* 1–4.

Michael, J. (1988) "Establishing Operations and the Mand." *The Analysis of Verbal Behavior, 6,* 3–9.

Miguel, C.F., Carr, J.E. and Michael, J. (2002) "The Effects of a Stimulus-Stimulus Pairing Procedure on the Vocal Behavior of Children Diagnosed with Autism." *The Analysis of Verbal Behavior, 18,* 3–13.

Mirenda, P. (2002) "Toward Functional Augmentative and Alternative Communication for Students with Autism: Manual Signs, Graphic Symbols, and Voice Output Communication Aids." *Language, Speech, and Hearing Services in Schools, 34,* 203–216.

Partington, J.W. and Sundberg, M.L. (1998) *The Assessment of Basic Language and Learning Skills.* Pleasant Hill, CA: Behavior Analysts, Inc.

Partington, J.W. and Sundberg, M.L. (1998) *The Assessment of Basic Language and Learning Skills: Scoring instructions and IEP Development Guide.* Pleasant Hill, CA: Behavior Analysts, Inc.

Pennsylvania Verbal Behavior Project (2006) *Family Handbook.* Retrieved September 25, 2006 from: http://www.pattan.net/files/Autism/VerbalBeh0106.pdf

Potter, B., and Brown, D. (1997) "A Review of Studies Examining the Nature of Selection-based and Topography-based Verbal Behavior." *The Analysis of Verbal Behavior, 14,* 85–103.

Shafer, E. (1994) "A review of Interventions to Teach a Mand Repertoire." The Analysis of Verbal Behavior, *12,* 53–66.

Skinner, B.F. (1953) *Science and Human Behavior.* New York: Macmillan.

Skinner, B.F. (1957) *Verbal Behavior.* New York: Appleton-Century.

Sundberg, M. and Michael, J. (2001) "The Benefits of Skinner's Analysis of Verbal Behavior for Children with Autism." *Behavior Modification, 25,* 698–724.

Sundberg, M.L., Michael, J., Partington, J.W. and Sundberg, C.A. (1996) "The role of Automatic Reinforcement in Early Language Acquisition." *The Analysis of Verbal Behavior, 13,* 21–37.

Sundberg, M.L. and Partington, J.W. (1998) *Teaching Language to Children with Autism or Other Developmental Disabilities.* California: Behavior Analysts, Inc.

Sundberg, M. and Partington, J. (2001) *Behavior Analysts Quick Tips. Behavior Teaching Strategies,* Pleasant Hill, CA: Behavior Analysts, Inc.

Vail, T., Freeman, D. and Peters, C. (2002) *Mariposa School Employee Training Manual.* Retrieved September 1, 2006 from: http://www.mariposaschool.org/programs/TrainingManual.pdf

Van Pelt, K. (1988) *Potty Training Your Baby.* Garden City Park, NY: Avery Pulishing Group, Inc.

Watson, T.S. and Steege, M.W. (2003) *Conducting School-Based Functional Behavioral Assessments: A Practitioners Guide.* New York: Guilford.

Weiss, M.J.and Delmolino, L. (2006) "The Relationship between Early Learning Rates and Treatment Outcome for Children with Autism Receiving Intensive Home-based Applied Behavior Analysis." *The Behavior Analyst Today, 7,* 96–110.

Wheeler, M. (1998) *Toilet Training for Individuals with Autism and Related Disabilities.* Arlington, TX: Future Horizons.

Williams, G. and Greer, R.D. (1993) "A Comparison of Verbal-behavior and Linguistic-communication Curricula for Training Developmentally Delayed Adolescents to Acquire and Maintain Vocal Speech." *Behaviorology, 1,* 31–46.

Wiseman, N.D. (2006) *Could it be Autism? A Parent's Guide to the First Signs and Next Steps.* New York: Broadway Books.

Woolery, M., Ault, M.J. and Doyle, P.M. (1992) *Teaching Students with Moderate to Severe Disabilities.* White Plains, NY: Longman.

Index